Deep Waters

Detail from *Indian Cabin at Deep River* by Catherine de Grey
(acrylic on beaverboard, autumn 1947)

Deep Waters

The Ottawa River and Canada's
Nuclear Adventure

Kim Krenz

McGill-Queen's University Press
Montreal & Kingston · London · Ithaca

Legal deposit second quarter 2004
Bibliothèque nationale du Québec

Printed in Canada on acid-free paper that is 100% ancient forest free (100%
post-consumer recycled), processed chlorine free.

McGill-Queen's University Press acknowledges the support of the
Canada Council for the Arts for our publishing program. We also acnowl-
edge the financial support of the Government of Canada through the
Book Publishing Industry Development Program (BPIDP) for our publishing activities.

National Library of Canada Cataloguing in Publication

Krenz, F. H. Kim (Ferdinand Henry Kim), 1920–
Deep waters : the Ottawa River and Canada's nuclear adventure /
F.H. Kim Krenz.
Includes bibliographical references and index.
ISBN 0-7735-2691-9
1. Nuclear energy–Research–Ontario–Deep River Region–History.
2. Chalk River Nuclear Laboratories–History. 3. CANDU Reactor–History.
4. Deep River (Ont.)–History. I. Title.

TK1347.O5K74 2004   621.48'09713'81   C2003-905904-9

This book was designed by Mantz/Eiser graphic design and typeset
in 11/15.5 John Baskerville

*To Kate, without whom none of this would have
happened to me; and to the memory
of R.F.S. (Bob) Robertson and to the many friends
and colleagues, present or departed,
who shared this story.*

Contents

Illustrations
ix

Acknowledgments
xi

The Deep River Song
xiii

Introduction
3

1 Beginnings
13

2 Loggers into Technicians
39

3 Wartime Secrecy
61

4 Nuclear Reactors
76

5 Nuclear Applications
91

6 Nuclear Power
110

Epilogue: Nuclear Critics
136

References
157

Index
165

Illustrations

Frontispiece   detail from *Indian Cabin at Deep River*,
Catherine de Grey, 1947

Comment on transportation to the plant,
Kim Krenz, 1946   20

NRC and DIL, excerpt from the *Deep River
Review*, 1946   23

Arms Race, a poem by Chris Reid, 1946   28

Pine Point above Deep River, Catherine
de Grey, 1947   37

Map of the Gillies Brothers' timber limits in the
Ottawa Valley, ca 1920   42

Plutonium Pete, excerpt from the
Deep River Review, 1946   47

W.B. Lewis at the unveiling of the
ZEEP plaque, 1966   82

Chalk River Laboratories at night,
1966 87

The first fueling machine for NPD, 1963 119

Panoramic view of NPD, 1964 120

Photographs at 300°C and 100 p.s.i.,
ca 1960 126

J.L. Gray with the Vaniers at Chalk
River, 1966 140

W.B. Lewis at the head of the pack, 1977 155

Acknowledgments

Some twenty years have elapsed since I was actively engaged in the field of nuclear energy, and twice that since Kate and I lived in Deep River. Some details have become confused and some memories have dimmed since those early days during and just after World War II. In putting this story together I have referred to others for criticism, correction, or corroboration. My special thanks are due to Dr Lorne G. McConnell and his wife, Dora, for reading the earlier texts and supplying extensive corrections and a detailed commentary. Dr J. Terry Rogers has been indefatigable in reading versions of the text and making further corrections and suggestions. I am much indebted to him for information on recent developments. Our close friends Bill and Dorothy Prosser have gone through at least two versions with a jaundiced eye, Dorothy not only as one of the original members of the Montreal group but as a retired teacher of Canadian literature to boot. Helen Bajorek MacDonald, a colleague at Trent, feminist, and nuclear critic, provided useful insights into the work. Joan Melvin of Deep River, an experienced writer and editor, whose history of that town has been a source of inspiration, gave pointed criticism and good advice. My thanks to Catherine de Grey for allowing me to use a detail from her painting of an Indian cabin on the Ottawa River; to

Catherine de Grey and Dorothy Prosser for permission to reprint from the *Deep River Review*; to Atomic Energy of Canada Limited for permission to use photographs from AECL annual reports; to Ralph S. Flemons and GE Canada for two photographs; to *Nuclear Engeneering International* for permission to use a cartoon from the cover of the journal.

Michael Harrison, submissions editor of Broadview Press, himself of Deep River origin, put me and the manuscript on the right track for publication. Lesley Barry of McGill-Queen's University Press has been an invaluable confederate in bringing the manuscript to its final form. Finally, my wife, Kate, has been my personal treasure, without whom none of this could have happened. I am indebted to all of these people, but have at times adhered stubbornly to my own version of events. I am therefore by no means "off the hook."

Lakefield, Ontario

July 2003

The Deep River Song

Since the day Deep River blessed this barren shore
We b'en happy like we never were before.
No more choppin' ice and wood; we can now enjoy the good
Of Atomic Energy.
Chorus   *Of Atomic Energy, my boys, of Atomic Energy.*
No more choppin' ice or wood; we can now enjoy the good
Of Atomic Energy.

Oh, I used to roll the logs for Gillies Bros.,
But I don't do that no more because
I got a job down at the Plant with a scientific slant
Workin' on Atomic Energy!
Chorus   *Workin' on Atomic Energy, my boys, workin' on Atomic Energy.*
I've got a job down at the Plant with a scientific slant
Workin' on Atomic Energy.

Well, the boys down at the Plant, they made me swear
That I'd never tell you what goes on down there.
But shovellin' sand for sixty cents is just the same inside a fence
Workin' on Atomic Energy.
Chorus   *Workin' on Atomic Energy, my boys, workin' on Atomic Energy.*
Shovellin' sand for sixty cents is just the same inside a fence
Workin' on Atomic Energy.

They've a thing they call the "pile" at the Plant.
Well, I'd like to say I've seen it, but I can't.
They say that when she really goes all the boys take off
*   their clothes*
And enjoy Atomic Energy!
Chorus   *And enjoy Atomic Energy, my boys, and enjoy Atomic Energy.*
They say that when she really goes all the boys take off
*   their clothes*
And enjoy Atomic Energy!

Oh, the day, the day, the happy, happy day
When I buy my "One Horse Atom Shay."
I'll "pull the rods" and let her go off to Pembroke through
*   the snow,*
Runnin' on Atomic Energy!

Chorus   *Runnin' on Atomic Energy, my boys, runnin' on Atomic Energy.*
I'll "pull the rods" and let her go off to Pembroke through
*   the snow*
Runnin' on Atomic Energy!

Now the moral of my story is not far.
If you ever want to buy an atom car,
You must really take a lease on an everlasting peace;
Never use this Energy for war!

Chorus   *Never use this Energy for war, my boys, never use this Energy*
*   for war.*
You must really take a lease on an everlasting peace;
Never use this Energy for war!

This song was written and performed by me at the Deep River Community Centre in the winter of 1947 at a variety show to commemorate the first two years of the village of Deep River.

Deep Waters

Introduction

I have been advised by those more knowledgeable than myself to preface these musings and reminiscences with an introduction. I will begin therefore with the statement that I have always been mildly surprised at the course my life has taken. I do not really know, for instance, how I came to be involved in atomic energy. It was during the Second World War and I was enrolled in the Ph.D. program at the University of Toronto. Even being in Toronto was something of a surprise, for I had been brought up in an American family in Peking, China, where I graduated from the Peking American School, a devoted disciple – as were all the other graduates – of Alice F. Moore, the American principal. This unusual institution was one of the first truly international schools, drawing its student body from American and Chinese families and the international diplomatic community of Peking. There were also children from the large number of White Russian families living in Peking.

My parents had separated and the family was supported by my mother and her sister, who worked as stenographers and secretaries in the American embassy in Peking. I came to the University of Rochester in upstate New York in 1937 as a Genesee Scholar, and was granted, after four years (and somewhat reluctantly), a B.Sc. in chemistry by that university.

The sojourn in Rochester had been lonely and very far from home until close friends of my aunt in Canada took me in, gave me work during the summer months, and eventually introduced me to the Canadian girl who was to become my wife. Kate's family provided an entrée into life in Canada. As soon as I had my degree from Rochester, we were married in Toronto, and I applied and was accepted into the Ph.D. program in chemistry at the university there.

Meanwhile the world had been shaken again and again by events seemingly beyond anyone's control. My departure from Peking had been precipitated by the Japanese invasion of north China, and a brief visit to Peking during my sophomore summer at Rochester convinced me that a clash between Japan and the United States was imminent. In September 1939, as I was returning to Rochester, war was declared between Great Britain and Germany, and Canada was swept almost immediately into the conflict.

As Canada became immersed in the war effort, those of us in science at the University of Toronto did war work in parallel to our thesis work in the Department of Chemistry. The attack by the Japanese on Pearl Harbor brought an unwelcome fulfillment of my premonition of war in Asia. My mother and aunt and the younger of my two sisters were interned by the Japanese in the embassy compound in Peking and for months I was uncertain as to their fate, although I was advised that they would be repatriated on the first transfer of diplomatic prisoners. My older sister was at college in Boston. I had been called up by the Canadian army in 1944 and had gone through indoctrination at the No. 1 Manning Depot in the "Horse Palace" in the Canadian National Exhibition grounds in Toronto. I thought I had done rather well on the M-Test and was thinking of applying for officer training. A colleague in the department, Syd Barnartt, had already become a full-fledged lieutenant. My thesis work at the University of Toronto was not going well.

At this point Kate and I received in our apartment an unannounced and unexpected visit from a Dr Hill, a medical doctor attached to a secret project in Montreal. Dr Hill advised us to pack up and move to Montreal as quickly as possible as I was to join the project as an employee of Defence Industries Limited, or DIL. This was a wartime branch of Canadian Industries Limited, which was, as I learned later, itself a branch plant of Imperial Chemical Industries Limited in England. During World War II DIL operated on contract with the Department of Munitions and Supply, producing explosives for the war effort.

Dr Hill seemed very nervous and tense. He could not say anything about the project except that "the scientists have learned how to split the atom." At the time I had no idea what this implied. The idea of joining a secret project in Montreal seemed attractive, however, and Kate and I said we would go.

It seems disloyal to Kate's extended family in Toronto who were so kind to us, but I must confess that the move from Toronto to Montreal, even in wartime, was like a move from night into day. We found Montreal charming. My mother, repatriated with the first exchange of diplomatic prisoners from China as promised, had been posted to Montreal, where she had an elegant apartment on Peel Street. She happily took us in, and we stayed with her as long as we were in Montreal.

In April 1945, I reported to DIL head office at 625 Dorchester (now Blvd René Lévesque) and found I was to be assigned to a group of scientists and technicians working at what was called the Montreal Laboratory, in the newly built University of Montreal. I was warned by Gordie Hatfield, a senior DIL manager, that the scientists were a "pretty hairy bunch." The DIL team, he advised, was composed of "regular guys" like Hatfield and, by implication, myself.

The Montreal Laboratory was the outcome of decisions among the U.S., Britain, and Canada to parcel out the work to be done by the three countries in the field of atomic energy. Britain was already contributing to projects in the United States, but wished to carry on work on heavy water reactors begun at the Cavendish Laboratory in England. With the agreement of the three countries, the Montreal Laboratory had been established in 1942 to research and produce the design for a heavy water nuclear reactor for generating plutonium, the nuclear explosive. Established as an Atomic Energy Project administrated by Canada's National Research Council, the Montreal Laboratory had originally been housed in two private homes in Montreal with a few Canadian staff from the Research Council and a small group of English and European scientists, all of whom had done ground-breaking work in the fields of nuclear physics and chemistry. The Project grew rapidly, so that by early 1945, when I joined the Laboratory, it had taken over an entire wing of the University of Montreal and the staff had expanded to include nearly one hundred British scientists and engineers.

Security was tight at 625 Dorchester and at the Laboratory, surveillance and control being supplied by the Royal Canadian Mounted Police. RCMP clearance was required for all Canadians. As an American, I had rather special status, for the Project depended heavily upon the United States for technical help and information. I nevertheless had to be cleared by the RCMP, although since my father was a U.S. Marine and my mother an employee of the U.S. State Department, this was not a problem.

My first contact with the Project was in an interview with Dr G.C. Laurence, who had the task of inducting all Canadians. I do not remember much of the interview except for Laurence's pontificating on the need to appreciate the implications of heat diffusion mathematics, a somewhat surprising line to take in view of the fact that I was to help develop instruments for the detection of radiations from radioactive substances. I soon found that, far from being a "pretty hairy bunch," the scientists were a particularly interesting and attractive group of people; the presence of so many well-known scientific names added lustre to the excitement of participating in the Project. I began to suspect that the "hairy" scientists might perhaps even be more agreeable company than the "regular guys" promoted by Gordie Hatfield. Fortunately, I was noticed by Dr E.W.R. Steacie, deputy director of the Project and head of the Chemistry Department at McGill University in Montreal. He looked upon me as a "virtual Ph.D." and suggested that I transfer from DIL to the National Research Council. This was effected without difficulty, though it may have left a sour taste in some quarters of DIL.

It was as a research scientist with the Research Council that I spent the early years of the Project, first in Montreal and then at the Chalk River Nuclear Laboratories (now simply the Chalk River Laboratories) on the Ottawa River. In 1945 Kate and I moved from the apartment in Montreal to Deep River, the village on the Ottawa built for the Project employees. This was an entirely new experience for us, as it was for everyone else. The village had literally been "hacked out of the bush," and life took on many new features for the mostly urban dwellers that we were. Life in the village had imposed upon it the secrecy and security that characterized the Project, and this produced a special kind of intimacy among the 200 or so scientists, engineers, and technicians on the staff. We lived and worked within fenced and guarded enclosures, a captive, but privileged, society.

I had the good fortune to work under Dr Nicholas Miller, who in 1948 moved to the University of Edinburgh, where he established a radiation chemistry laboratory in the physics department of the university. The following year, he asked me to join him, and Kate and I spent several pleasant years in Edinburgh, becoming in the process ardent admirers of the Scots and things Scottish. I had by now won Canadian citizenship, however, and Canada was our home. We duly returned therefore to Deep River in 1955. As there was no post available in Radiation Chemistry, I was invited to transfer to work in Chemistry and Metallurgy, where new alloys were being developed for the nuclear power program. This was a fascinating field and, thanks to the Ph.D. I had gained from the Edinburgh experience, I was given a position of some responsibility. Things went well at first, but as the pressure of work increased it became apparent that I was not sufficiently grounded in the field to keep up with the rapid theoretical developments. Besides, my talents – such as they were – lay in the direction of technology rather than theory. When an opportunity arose in 1962 to represent Canada abroad, I seized it.

There followed two years in Europe where I was Canada's liaison scientist to Euratom, the atomic energy organization of the European Common Market. This involved getting to know the European programs inside and out, as well as directing development work at the Euratom Research Centre at Ispra in Italy. We lived in the beautiful Italian countryside within sight of the Alps.

I had been left pretty much on my own and "ran my own show," so that when I was due to return to the laboratory in Chalk River, I found the idea stultifying and asked for something else. A one-year appointment in Ottawa as head of International Affairs at the Atomic Energy of Canada Limited (AECL) head office became available for which my experience in Europe seemed to qualify me. The incumbent was taking leave of absence. I took on the job and learned a great deal about the workings of government in Ottawa. I also used the position and my contacts in Europe to promote internationally the Canadian nuclear power concept, CANDU, which I was convinced was superior to what the Americans and British were offering. Lorne Gray, who was then president of AECL, listened but did not feel the company was ready to embark upon sales of CANDUs in competition with offerings from General Electric, Westinghouse, or British suppliers.

Canadian General Electric was evidently prepared to do just that. Its Civilian Atomic Power Department in Peterborough was gearing up to promote Canadian nuclear expertise around the world. Unlike AECL, it could draw on a fund of marketing experience and techniques from the parent company in the United States. I was attracted, and arranged in 1966 for a transfer from AECL to the Peterborough company. The outcome of this adventure is described in the text of *Deep Waters*.

There followed a period in which I taught science in a small private school in Lakefield, Ontario; this was a particularly rewarding experience for both Kate and myself, as our marriage was never blessed with children. We will always feel that we owe the boys in that school more than we can ever repay, for the experience gave us an understanding of – and affection for – youth that we could not have gained in any other way.

Seven years as a teacher seemed enough, however, and I returned eventually to AECL as head of public education in the head office in Ottawa. It became a challenging position. This was the mid-1970s and AECL was being criticized both publicly and from within government. The anti-nuclear movement was reaching its zenith in the public forum and whole departments within government, such as the Energy Conservation Branch in the Ministry of Energy, Mines, and Resources, were attempting to undermine AECL's program of nuclear power development with every means at their disposal. David Brooks, an American influenced by the negative attitude toward nuclear development in the United States, was branch head of Energy Conservation, and the branch had attracted a whole new generation of young activists, some of whom did not hesitate to collaborate with like-minded people in the public sector, even at the risk of breaching government confidentiality.

I felt in time that I was coming to grips with the situation until an incident at a dance at the Rideau Club in Ottawa demonstrated to me the limitations of my influence. Kate and I attended the dance as guests of John Foster, the new president of AECL, and his wife, Margaret. The wife of a rather important government official began taking John to task for putting the Canadian public at risk with AECL's nuclear program. John was taken aback by an attack from this direction, particularly at a pleasant and relaxed social gathering, and seemed at a loss for words. I, on the other hand, had been dealing with public questions for the past year and could clearly see the answers needed to this lady's criticism. I tried to intervene to help John, but was stopped imperiously by the lady. *She wanted to hear it from the president.*

Perhaps I should have been philosophical about the incident, but somehow it triggered a response that had been growing in my mind. I arranged to be transferred on loan to the Energy Project of the National Research Council in Ottawa and spent an educational two years learning about the limitations of the much vaunted "renewable energy alternatives" and even more about the inefficiencies of projects involving more than one federal government department. In the end, I took early retirement in 1980 from AECL and, with Kate, started Abrico Energy Management Services, to help clients reduce their energy bills and to apply, where feasible, alternative energy strategies such as solar and wind installations. This led to an adventure of some ten years in which major projects were completed in Peterborough and in Barbados. Finally, when I turned seventy, it seemed time to withdraw from active life. I had a small pension from AECL and my wife a modest income from an estate left by her parents. We had a home in historic Lakefield and a circle of very congenial friends.

We were prepared to subside comfortably into local life in Lakefield when I was invited to become an external research associate of Trent University in nearby Peterborough. As my work at the university did not involve atomic energy in any sense, it will not be reported here. Once again, however, I found myself deeply indebted to young people and young minds for constant stimulation and inspiration.

———

I have been fortunate in the turns my life has taken. My marriage to Kate has provided me with a partner and the closest of friends for over sixty years. Each phase of our lives together has given us interests and challenges and opportunities for new friendships. The most memorable phase, though, is that early period when I was a member of the little band of scientists and engineers on the shore of the Ottawa River, working to develop useful power from a completely new source of energy, the atom. Their success is surely one of the great technical achievements of the twentieth century, and their story is an important part of recent Canadian history.

Canada's transformation from a very junior player in scientific and technical developments in the Second World War into the home of world class nuclear research and development facilities was a complex process, and this process has been ably described by scholarly historians. This book is, instead, an informal, first-hand account of the early days of the Canadian atomic energy project and of those principal events that led to the development of CANDU. While existing histories of the nuclear industry focus on its technical, economic, or political aspects, I have tried, albeit in an amateurish way, to deal with the psychological aspects of atomic energy.

I have tried, too, to tell this story in terms that are interesting to the general reader, for it is as much his or her story as it is mine. The implications of the use of atomic energy are enormous and it is not surprising that atomic energy has inspired as much dread and fear in some as it has inspired optimistic anticipation and growing confidence in others. My intention, therefore, has also been to tell the story in human terms, bringing the reader on a personal journey to an understanding of the matters at issue. It is an understanding badly needed by Canadians, who, in the months and years to come, will have to rely on CANDU for much of their electricity.

1

Beginnings

"Since the day Deep River blessed this barren shore
We be'en happy like we never were before.
No more choppin' ice and wood, we can now enjoy the good
Of Atomic Energy!"

The Deep River Song

Deep River is on the Ontario shore of the Ottawa River at a
point where the river is over a mile wide. The Ottawa is one of
the great rivers of Canada. If one looks through field glass-
es down the river from Fraser's Landing toward the narrows
above Oiseau Rock one can detect the curvature of the Earth.
Flowing from Lake Temiskaming in the northwest to the Lake
of Two Mountains in the southeast, the river forms 400 miles of
the interprovincial boundary between Ontario and Quebec.
For the most part it follows a geological fault along the edge of
the Laurentian highlands, which thrust up a series of cliffs and
fjords along the Quebec shore. The Ontario shore is generally
low-lying and slopes downward toward the base of the fault; in
places where the cliffs drop sheer into the river the water is very
deep. Measurements made during a 1944 federal survey at the
base of Oiseau Rock on the Quebec shore, several miles downstream from Deep River, show depths greater than a thousand
feet. At Deep River itself, the river is no deeper than eighty feet
in the main channel, and there are extensive shallows among
the bays and inlets on the Ontario side.

Deep River used to be a cluster of rough cabins among the
towering white pines on the Ontario shore. In the years leading up to World War II, the inhabitants were two or three fam-

ilies of Indians, living mainly on trapping, fishing, and hunting. Quebec across the river was an unspoiled wilderness teeming with game and wildlife, stretching unbroken a hundred miles to the east and the north. The men spent the winter over in Quebec, trapping and hunting under the harshest and most primitive conditions. Old Mr Huckabone, a local historian, told me the story of Mrs Jacobs, who accompanied her husband and froze to death in camp one particularly severe winter while Jacobs was out on the trapline. He stood her up in the snow beside the tent until the spring, when he could bring her out with the load of furs. For years I would often think of her, standing silent and alone in the snow, her presence brooding over the empty camp.

The men brought their furs out in the spring to Deep River, to be sold to the local fur trader, who would meet them at the beach with a case of whiskey. Transactions would be carried on in an atmosphere of uncontrolled conviviality and next day each Indian child would have a ten-dollar bill. Within a week all the money would be gone, and life among the families would resume its normal tenor until the following winter, when the cycle would repeat.

This cycle of events was interrupted, like so much else, by the war. Far from Deep River and the magnificent sweep of the Ottawa on which it looked, developments in politics and science had been progressing at an ever increasing pace toward a cataclysm in Europe that would change Canada, and Deep River with it, forever. Not that Canadian Aboriginals were unaware of Europe. Many from the Ottawa Valley had served with the Canadian forces in World War I. Some had served with distinction and returned with decorations for valour. Sadly, very little of this was reflected in their social status after the war. As one of them said, "When I was in Europe I was a Canadian. Now I am back in Canada, I am an Indian." The next generation of young native people, educated in Western ways, had yet to emerge from the schools and universities to demand their proper rights and status.

The white communities in the Ottawa Valley to which the demobilized soldiers of World War I had returned were a colourful mixture of Scots, Irish, and *Canadiens*. The Valley retains to this day a strong and characteristic accent in speaking English, delightfully garnished with phrases that are purely Irish and occasionally breaking into constructions that are unmistakably French: "You watch yourself, I'm gonna tell you some*thing*." Along the river itself French is spoken with facility, but it is a French in which many words and place names are given a pronunciation quite unknown in the colleges and seminaries of Quebec. "L'Oiseau," for instance, is pronounced "l'Weeso." Family names give no indication of racial origin, for a Murphy or a MacDonald may be just as *Canadien* as a Madore or a Mercereau.

The history of the Valley that produced this intriguing blend of language and culture is as rich as that in any part of Canada. What brought the Scots and Irish to the Valley was timber. The first settler to homestead in the region of what is now Hull, in Quebec across from the city of Ottawa, was Philemon Wright, who in 1800, at the age of forty, led a small group of Loyalists from Massachussetts to the Valley. In those days, one could not see more than fifty yards in any direction for the dense stands of virgin white pine. To climb one of these great trees, Wright had first to fell a smaller tree against the trunk so that he could reach the lower branches of the giant. Once at the top, he could look out over the Valley. The view that greeted him was of a forest of white and red pine stretching unbroken for forty miles to the horizon, the ridges dominated by great white pines, their dark green boughs extended in graceful arabesques to the lee of the prevailing wind. This was to be the source of wealth of the Gilmours, the Booths, the Bronsons, the Gillies, and many others. The Scots led the development of the industry with a shrewd eye to business. The Irish supplied the muscle and the French the knowledge of the country. Even after World War I, the business of felling white pine and sawing timber was a major industry.

But, as with all things, as there was a beginning there had to be an end. The last rafts of squared timbers were floated down the Ottawa River past the nation's capital in the early 1920s. Very few timber firms survived the Great Depression that followed, and those that did, like Gillies Brothers of Arnprior, survived by specializing in a limited range of lumber. Charlotte Whitton, scholar, political activist, and once secretary to Mr David Gillies, wrote a history of the company and the region with the title *A Hundred Years A'Fellin'*. She went on to become the mayor of Ottawa and the first woman mayor of any Canadian city. Small and pugnacious, she used to say that "You have to be twice as good as any man to get a man's job." Then she would add, "Fortunately, it's not difficult."

———————

Communities in the Ottawa Valley, like communities elsewhere in Canada, survived the Depression, but it was not easy. Highway 17 between Pembroke and North Bay was put through as a gravel road in 1937 by gangs of men working for twenty-five cents a day and living in tents in the dead of winter. It skirted the Canadian military base at Petawawa and led past Chalk River, a division point on the Canadian Pacific transcontinental railway line, and then veered away toward the Ottawa River where, at Father McElligott's little Catholic church, it came within two hundred yards of Deep River. It then proceeded northwest to Mattawa, more or less following the river, and finally on to North Bay. For several years, even after the declaration of war in 1939, there was not much traffic on the highway. One could drive for half an hour without meeting another car or truck.

With World War II, however, things began to change. Canadian Forces Base Petawawa sprang to life out of somnolence, as regional regiments throughout eastern Canada started to recruit and train. Both the Canadian Pacific and Canadian National railway lines began to hum with activity.

A University of Toronto economist, Lorne Morgan, was sufficiently impressed by the transformation in the Canadian National, once a "white elephant," now "trumpeting triumphantly across the country," that he produced a slim and sardonic little pamphlet entitled "Homo The Sap: Or The Perpetual War" in which he advocated, on the strength of then current evidence, that Canada should be engaged in a perpetual war, since this seemed a promising route to prosperity under capitalism. Col. W.E. Phillips, a prominent Toronto industrialist, had just been appointed chairman of the board of governors of the university, however, and nothing further was heard from Prof. Morgan.

The residual white pine industry furnished lumber for the construction of plants and company towns and supplied wood for a variety of uses. After the entry of the United States into the war, demand for Canadian lumber increased to the point where a system of control had to be developed, with British war needs first, U.S. war needs second, and Canadian war needs third. Lumber for peacetime uses was practically unavailable. My wife's sister built her family's first summer cottage out of used packing cases for aircraft components. The war benefitted the timber industry, as it did most others, but lumber faded in importance compared to the production of arms and explosives and the movement of men and articles of war. Pembroke, which had been an important centre of the timber industry, was effectively bypassed by this activity, and even during the war years considered thirty cents an hour a good wage. Chalk River benefitted from the railway, though it did not have to expand appreciably. Deep River remained much as it had always been, but great changes were in the wings.

Without warning – the local municipal and county councils would become accustomed to this kind of treatment – the Canadian government expropriated thousands of acres of land on the river about six miles from the small inland settlement of Chalk River, along with a further large tract at Deep River. Rumours flew as to what was afoot. Those with inside information let it be known that a wartime polymer plant was to be built at the first site and that the second site was to be used for housing the workers. The whole matter was a wartime secret, and one of the first actions at each site was to build exclusion fences topped with barbed wire and place security guards at the entrances. Within the second enclosure, at the Deep River site, German prisoners of war were brought in to clear off the secondary growth that, aside from the pines at the water's edge, covered the area. The plant site included the Felix Beauchamp cattle farm and was largely clear of brush.

The Indian families at Deep River were moved into the country along the Wiley Road toward the Canadian Pacific track. The original residents at both sites were to some extent compensated and encouraged to join the construction workforce. It soon became public knowledge that the government was constrained by law to pay a minimum wage of fifty-seven cents an hour. The countryside became drained of manpower, for everyone wanted to join the construction workforce. A deputation from the Pembroke chamber of commerce complained bitterly to the management at the site that no one in Pembroke wanted to work for the generous sum of thirty-five cents an hour and that a higher rate would drive them out of business. It is a matter of record, however, that most of the businesses survived and many, in fact, prospered in the post-war years. In any event, there was nothing the management could do. As a government operation its hands were tied.

Workers were brought in from Pembroke to both the plant and the townsite in wooden vehicles that looked like cattle cars, without windows, and each drawn by a heavy truck. Seats ran down either side and a stove in the middle provided heat in the winter. What would have happened had one of these run off the road is dreadful to imagine, but no such accident was ever reported. The highway from Pembroke was now paved to just beyond Petawawa, but remained a gravel road from there on. There was minimum springing in these vehicles, and the thirty-two-mile ride to the settlement at Chalk River must have been bone-shaking. There was then a further six miles of plant road from "Chalk" to the plant, if anything worse than the highway. Workers arrived at 7 a.m. after a drive of at least an hour and a half, so breakfasted, if at all, at 5 o'clock. The shift ended at 4 p.m., when the return trip to Pembroke was made.

There were workers from the surrounding countryside as well, mostly men who were accustomed to working in the bush. Farms were few and far between, the land on the Ontario side being mainly sand from what was once many thousands of years ago the floor of the Champlain Sea. Repeated ridges of sand bars are still in evidence around Chalk River. The poor soil was said to be suitable only for potatoes, but even potatoes were a dubious crop. Ancient, abandoned farms with tumble-down log buildings were a feature of the landscape. These farms had been cleared of trees early in the nineteenth century by English settlers, many of them half-pay officers from the army, in the vain hope that a new life as farmers was the way of the future. Any Scot could have told them the land was good only for trees, and only for spruce and pine at that. The abundance of flourishing evergreens gives the region a special character, which greets the visitor the moment he unlatches his car door and steps into the open. The air is filled with the resinous perfume of pines. This was the reward to the weary traveler coming to Chalk River from Montreal or Ottawa on

"Don't ask me why, dear, but they do it twice a day."

A commentary on transportation to the plant. A cartoon by Kim Krenz published in the July 1946 edition of the *Deep River Review*. By special permission of the *Deep River Review*.

the Canadian Pacific transcontinental, which pulled into Chalk River Station at 11:30 in the evening. After hours cooped up in a carriage smelling of soot, dirty upholstery, and the overheated surfaces of the clanging steam pipes, he or she could step out into the cold, clean night air, redolent with the perfume of evergreens.

––––––––––.

The decision had been made to turn management and operations of the plant over to Defence Industries Limited. DIL, as it was known, had been charged early in the war with the construction and operation of an explosives plant at Nobel, near Parry Sound, Ontario. The work of construction of the plant at Chalk River was done by Fraser Brace Construction. By the time this work had started, Nobel was winding down and DIL staff and office equipment were being transferred to Chalk River.

Unknown to the local inhabitants of the Valley and to the general public, the facilities being constructed were for a secret project administered by the National Research Council of Canada (NRC), based in Ottawa. The plant site had been chosen for its abundant cooling water from the Ottawa River, its remoteness from the centres of population, its approximate equidistance from Ottawa and Toronto, and its convenient closeness to a major railway line. In due course the Project, as it was known, was to accommodate not only staff from DIL and NRC but also a large contingent of British scientists and engineers who had been assigned to the project early in the war and had been working at the University of Montreal in what was known as the Montreal Laboratory.

DIL had developed a management system called "straight line organization," which had apparently worked well at Nobel. Decisions at each level were passed up the line of management before being made, a process that left the lower levels with lots of responsibility but limited authority, a situation perhaps desirable for those in senior management but poorly adapted to the experimental and innovative experience that the Chalk River Project was to become. It came into direct conflict with the ethos of the scientists from the National Research Council, who were to provide the scientific expertise for the project. As NRC was the lead organization, there was little hesitation on the part of some scientists to make life difficult for employees of DIL. From the standpoint of the latter, the scientists were a bunch of longhairs lacking discipline and control.

The situation worsened when scientists from England and France, who formed a major part of the project at the Montreal Laboratory, were transferred to the Chalk River Project. They tended to look upon all Canadians as somewhat backward and the Canadians of DIL as completely beyond the pale. Even the most junior of the Europeans had no hesitation in bearding Mr Desbarats, the project manager for DIL, on the slightest of matters. It was undoubtedly hard to take and led to a division that did nothing to smooth the development of the project. Individuals were categorized as being either DIL or NRC and treated accordingly. When Monty Finniston, the chief metallurgist of Tube Alloys in England, checked into the townsite Staff Hotel, he was asked immediately, "Are you DIL or NRC?" After a puzzled pause he said, "I'm Jewish."

It took some years before this unfortunate rift was smoothed over as it gradually became apparent to the scientists that there were many excellent people working for DIL. In my experience, those in DIL often returned the compliment.

————————

Canadians in those distant days were much more British than they are today, and there was - at least among older Canadians - a degree of deference to the mother country that would now be regarded as quaint and perhaps comical. The forceful infusion by circumstance of a group of young British scientists into a Canadian community of mostly young people - scien-

These cartoons by N. Quentin Lawrence of the U.K. contingent were published in the first issue of the *Deep River Review* of July 1946 as illustrations for a tongue-in-cheek article on Deep River by Maurice Lister. The article purports to be a review of the work of one Dr Wienerschnitzel, a sociologist and historian with an intimate knowledge of the period 1940–46, working in the year 2446.

Quoting from the *Review*: "...The community itself seems to have contained two sects, named N.R.C. and D.I.L. Dr Coriopsis of Dill University has explained these as 'Northwoods Recluse Congregation' and 'Devotees of the Inner Light,' and I incline to agree with him. Their difference in dogma is less certain. N.R.C. seems to have emphasized theory and theological faith; D.I.L. specialized in works..."

(And in a footnote) "Figs. 1 and 2 are reprinted by courtesy of Dr Wienerschnitzel...Fig. 1 shows the 'N.R.C. typus'; Fig. 2 the 'D.I.L. typus.' They are reconstructed from his intimate knowledge of the history of the period."

Note: Unfortunately the humour of Lister's article was lost on many of the Ottawa Valley residents, some of whom had advertised in the *Review*. They leapt to the conclusion that fig. 2 was an unflattering representation of the original inhabitants of the Valley and reacted with indignation and disgust. It was a harsh lesson for the budding editors of the journal.

tists, engineers, and others – brought about inevitable comparisons of culture and competence. It became apparent almost immediately that the young Brits were for the most part cultured intellectually beyond any of the young Canadians, even those with advanced university degrees. Quentin Lawrence, a tall, aristocratic young engineer with enormous RAF moustaches, would hold forth on the qualities of the music of Buxtehude quite honestly and without intention to impress. His Canadian counterpart would not only be blissfully ignorant of the existence of Buxtehude but probably be ignorant of classical music as well, certainly of seventeenth-century church cantatas. On the other hand the Brits often exhibited an attitude to the opposite sex that to the Canadians seemed adolescent to the point of childishness. A British education did indeed seem to "prolong adolescence into early manhood." Not that there were no humorous references to sex. Fay and Gill Organ, secretaries for the British contingent, were known among the Brits as "the female Organs." The Brits had never seen tea bags before and referred to them as "contraceptive tea." But it was evident that in a young and vigorous Canada matters of procreation were regarded far more seriously and with earlier application than in Britain.

In matters of technical competence there was less to separate the Canadians from the Brits. The same Quentin Lawrence was shown by a young engineer, Lorne McConnell, fresh out the Canadian Navy, that there were far more accurate ways to measure the speed of shut-down mechanisms than the one Lawrence was proposing. However, the Brits often showed a greater cultural depth in their field of specialization and tended to give greater meaning to the term "profession." This could well have resulted from the rigidity of class structures persisting in Britain to that time and the importance of defining oneself as belonging to a professional class. Some, like Prof. Fred Dainton, had strong convictions about the existence of an "intellectual aristocracy." The knighthood that he received later in his career must have done much to vindicate such a belief.

Manpower was at a premium during the years of the war and skilled manpower was almost unobtainable. It says a great deal for both DIL and Fraser Brace that they achieved what they did with the material that was at hand. Bulldozers were operated by men who had never driven anything larger than a farm tractor, and the ruined corner of the Fraser Brace field office became mute testimony to the learning process. Many of the carpenters hired to put together the housing in Deep River could not saw a straight cut or drive a nail. Instructions were a problem. Bilingualism was yet a future dream and many of those who were hired spoke Ottawa Valley French rather than English. Sign language became the rule, but even when highly developed it lacked the precision to explain what the boss really wanted. The level of education of most of the local workers who had grown up in the Depression was abysmal, though it must be added that this was no indicator of intelligence or competence. Lucien Côté, a local truck driver hired by Ian MacKay, head of the NRC engineering branch, transfered a 750-pound Volvo marine engine from its packing case on the truck into the hull and onto the engine bed of Ian's cruiser, using some lengths of chain and a crane-like structure fashioned from the trunks of jackpine trees (referred to by Lucien as "th' ole gin pole"); Ian claimed that Lucien had as good a grasp of engineering principles as many of his qualified engineers.

Then there were the ingrained *habitudes* characteristic of the Valley. In the spring men did not show up for work because it was the time for the spring drive and they took to the woods. The ranks of workers thinned again in the autumn when the deer hunt was on. The men were often brutal. Mealtimes in the Fraser Brace cafeteria were patrolled by armed guards after someone got a fork through the back of his hand when he reached for something another man wanted.

These and many other difficulties were overcome one by one, and in mid-August 1945, when the true nature of the Project came out, many of the major buildings at the plant were complete and operational and the Deep River townsite was recognizably a village, with streets, houses – some of which were being used as shops – a partially completed Staff Hotel, and a Community Centre. The town had been laid out tastefully by John Bland, professor of town planning at McGill, and care had been taken to preserve as many of the better trees as possible. Streets were named after early explorers and seigneurs – Frontenac, de Troyes, Iberville, Champlain – and after trees and features of the landscape.

The news was, of course, that the plant was not being built to produce polymers at all but was a major Canadian project in a completely new field of endeavour, tapping the energy available in the atom. Earlier in the month, Japan had surrendered to the Allies after atomic explosions at Hiroshima and Nagasaki had slaughtered or maimed hundreds of thousands of Japanese. The previous May, after the German surrender, Dr John D. Cockcroft, the scientific director of the Chalk River Project, had been part of a team sent by the victorious Allies to determine how far the Germans had progressed along this route. It was discovered that though Prof. Werner Heisenberg, a prominent scientist, had been put in charge of the German project, Hitler had given it scant priority, preferring to put his faith in buzz bombs and rockets. Thus, the United States and, with it, the Canadian international project were in the unique position of being far ahead of the rest of the world in the field of atomic energy. The fear that this frightening source of energy would fall into the hands of Hitler had been the moving force behind the American and Allied programs. That this did not happen and the fact that the energy had been used to inflict terrible damage on the unsuspecting Japanese were enough to turn many away from this field of work. Science in the service of victory for one's country at war was one thing; science for the sake of science when human welfare might be at stake was another. For Canadians, however, it became clear soon after the war that Canada was embarking on the development of the peaceful uses of atomic energy.

————.

Britain was particularly anxious to keep a team of experts in place. Their scientists stayed on at the Canadian project until the British government research centre at Harwell, near Oxford, could be readied for them; they contributed greatly to the furtherance of Canadian research and development. Dr Cockcroft was named director of the project at Harwell and was among the first British scientists to return home. He was knighted for his contributions to science and technology shortly thereafter and, with E.T.S. Walton, won the Nobel Prize for physics in 1952.

Cockcroft's presence had brought much scientific distinction to the project in Canada. One would not have guessed it from his appearance. Of somewhat less than medium height, wearing a battered fedora above a nondescript topcoat, he was easily passed over in a crowd. He had enormous powers of organization, however, and must have been able to hold simultaneously in his mind great amounts of disparate information. He had the ability to summarize in a sentence or two the essentials of the most complex arguments. It was humbling for someone giving a scientific paper to have Cockcroft recapitulate with great precision and few words what the lecturer had just spent an hour in saying. Bea Crossley, his secretary in Montreal and Chalk River, said she had never met anyone so well organized in the whole of her long experience.

Gerald Tooley, a chauffeur for NRC, used to drive Cockcroft on his later trips from Ottawa to Deep River or to the Chalk River Project. Gerald remarked that Sir John, who preferred the front seat beside the driver, often concealed a paper bag of

ARMS RACE

A Poem by Chris Reid

Scientist, brother, little savant,
Wave the nationalistic flag.
If you've brains – or if you haven't –
Even you can share the swag.
Protons, deuterons, whirl 'em around,
The job is good, the pay is sound.

Don't descend to tanks or mortars,
Lust to kill or smell of blood.
Science is pure and bright and shining,
Keeps us from the stench and mud.
Protons, deuterons, nights at the Ritz,
And soon we'll blow the world to bits.

Maybe fission bombs appal you,
Don't give up, we understand;
Go and work on fundamentals,
Ostrich head in college sand.
Protons, deuterons, lots of tricks;
The world can fry in politics.

You're the thinker, you're the purist,
Truth must out for good or bad.
Though conscience whispers words of caution
And laymen say "The utter cad!"
Protons, deuterons, graphite piles,
Then to bed or nights on the tiles.

Should we think of all the people
Living lives they can't repeat?
They have no simple wave equation,
Let us not become effete!
Protons, deuterons, take off the brakes,
We'll all be dead in a couple of shakes.

———

This poem was first published in the *Deep River Review* of
October 1946 and reflects honestly the unspoken thoughts
of many of us at that time. Chris was a chemist and member
of the UK contingent at Chalk River.

candies and would occasionally pop one in his mouth. "He never offered me one. Maybe he thought I couldn't see what he was doing." Cockcroft was not alone in keeping himself going with glucose lozenges. Peter Ustinov relates that he encountered the same thing when he visited Telecommunications Research Establishment in England while still in uniform. The "boffin" in charge (W.B. Lewis?) offered him a candy from a paper bag and found that he had two stuck together. "Oh, do take two," Ustinov was urged.

Despite the blandishments of the British government, many of the Britons returned to their pre-war careers in research and education. C.P. Snow, the British writer known for his examination of the chasm between popular and scientific cultures, was the chief instrument of British government persuasion. Not only were the major scientific figures on the British team not interested in government work, but many of the more junior scientists were not interested in leaving Canada. Prof. E.A. Guggenheim – *the* Prof. E.A. Guggenheim – tiny and vitriolic, with a crown of white curls, strode through the corridors of the laboratory in Montreal, accosting everyone he met with the expostulation "They want us to believe that service to the government is the highest calling there is. Well, I don't agree." Some young scientists, like Philip Tunnicliffe, actually left Canada for the Harwell project but eventually returned to Chalk River. His mind was made up the morning in England when he came down for breakfast in his Canadian parka with its hood up and said to his wife, "Pat, let's go back to Canada."

The expatriate English and Scots at Chalk River formed an important nucleus of scientists and engineers to which other British were attracted from time to time. Whether it was a matter of policy, or simply the availability of scientists and engineers in post-war Britain, the professional ranks of the Chalk River Project became noticeably British in the course of the years – so much so, in fact, that a student on a high school tour of the plant in the 1970s was heard to ask his teacher, "Sir, do you have to be English to work here?"

A small Free French team was also attached to the Canadian project during the war and made important contributions to the development of the Canadian reactor concept. Dr Lew Kowarski, who could play the piano with his back to the instrument and his hands crossed behind him, led the team of Canadians and New Zealanders that brought the first low power reactor into being at Chalk River.

One of the émigré Russians flourishing in Paris before the war, Kowarski brought a colourful and unmistakably Slavic presence to any gathering. To the casual observer he gave the impression of grossness; he was a large man with heavy, Slavic features topped with a brush cut. His appearance belied his shrewdness. He was, for instance, loath to come to Canada while his former colleague Hans von Halban was director of the international project in Montreal. In this Kowarski showed shrewd foresight, for von Halban was to become a major problem for the project. He was a poor administrator, autocratic and intransigent, and was suspected by the Americans of having communist sympathies. These problems were solved only by his removal and his replacement by Cockcroft. It is to von Halban's credit that he was ready to cooperate in any way he could to resolve the impasse. With von Halban out of the way, Kowarski readily joined the team in Montreal and was one of the first scientists to come to Chalk River. He, perhaps more than any other individual, set Canada on a course of developing natural uranium/heavy water reactors.

Kowarski published in 1947 an article on the evolution of large scientific research centres in the American journal *Bulletin of the Atomic Scientists* and predicted with uncanny accuracy the different stages through which such centres evolve, very much as Jacques describes the seven ages of man in Shakespeare's *As You Like It*. Kowarski also described with uncomfortable precision the types of individuals who flourish in such centres. One is what the French call a *fonctionaire*, an individual who makes no visible contribution to the advancement of the project yet who manages to be on all committees and delegations and at all photo opportunities. There are such individuals in every project of any importance, and the international project at the Montreal Laboratory was no exception. One representative of the Department of Munitions and Supply did not fit into any activity of the Montreal Laboratory, yet felt it his duty to tour the laboratory from time to time, if only, one supposes, to advertise his presence. He was the epitome of the faceless civil servant, colourless and formal, in an age when formality was the norm. Imagine his surprise and dismay, then, upon entering the chemistry counting room (where young women were making routine measurements of radioactivity) to find Bertrand Goldschmidt, the senior radiochemist, painting the beautiful legs of Eileen Little, the future Lady Fenning, with leg make-up. Our *fonctionaire* was transfixed, and backed slowly out of the room with his eyes fixed on those beautiful legs. He left the project shortly thereafter to take up another government position.

Goldschmidt, a French chemist who as a student had worked with Marie Curie in Paris, was another vivid figure, especially for the younger set at the Montreal Laboratory, who were shocked but delighted by his eccentricities. Coming from a wealthy Jewish family in Paris, he had been brought up by an English nanny, so spoke perfect English, larded with a Parisian accent. He had become uninsurable in Paris before the war owing to an accident when he was driving his car to a dinner engagement. Hurrying around a corner, he lost control of the car and smashed into a taxi that was parked in a taxi queue in the centre of the boulevard. Damage to his car and the taxi was total, and the next taxi in the queue was also damaged. Goldschmidt, still hurrying to his dinner, ran down the line of taxis, engaged an undamaged taxi at the end of the queue, and drove off to his dinner. He acknowledged that the insurance companies had a point in refusing to insure him, but relished in telling the tale.

It was not the fashion in the days when Marie Curie ruled the Institut de Radium in Paris to observe more than rudimentary precautions when handling radioactive material, and Goldschmidt could never bring himself to take seriously the sober regulations promulgated at Chalk River by the Health Radiation Branch. It was he who set off all the alarms in the gatehouse by walking through with a capsule containing 400 milligrams of radium, which should have been residing safely within a lead container in his laboratory, caught in his pant-cuff.

The French left the Montreal Laboratory and returned to Paris with the German surrender in May 1945. Goldschmidt and Kowarski stayed on at Chalk River, Kowarski to complete the work on the zero-energy reactor ZEEP and Goldschmidt to finish some work on chemical extraction. Both were therefore much in evidence during the formative days of the new community at Deep River. Goldschmidt in particular was a centre of interest to the French Canadian workmen who were building the Staff Hotel, none of whom had ever seen a real Frenchman. His electric shaver, the first to be used in Deep River, was an object of fascination to them all. Several reassured him of their Frenchness: *"Je n'oublie jamais, Monsieur, que je suis français même que vous."*

The late spring and summer of 1945 saw the community of Deep River beginning to take shape as a new village on the shore of the Ottawa River. In residence was a growing community of between fifty and one hundred scientists, engineers, and their families – Canadians, British, two New Zealanders who were part of the British contingent, and the two French scientists. They were mostly young and idealistic, mostly urban, many unmarried, most having advanced education, and most completely unaware of what the coming winter would have in store for them.

As part of the process of settlement it had been decided that the housing no longer needed at Nobel would be cut up, transported, and reassembled at Deep River. Cockcroft, in his notes made during an exploratory visit to Nobel, had referred to this as "nice colonial style housing for the staff." These constructions were known to us locally as "wartime fours" and "wartime sixes," simple four- and six-room wood-frame houses mounted on cement block foundations or, as in the case at Deep River, on cedar stakes embedded in the sand. Insulation was at a minimum, and at Deep River floor insulation for wartime housing was non-existent. This meant that floor temperatures reflected faithfully the outside temperature, even when heat sources in the dwelling were working at maximum capacity. In most homes these sources were a wood- or coal-burning stove in the kitchen and another in the centre of the dwelling. Temperature stratification in mid-winter was severe: floor temperatures hovered at some ten degrees below freezing while temperatures rose at waist level to a barely tolerable forty degrees Celsius. It was claimed by some that water placed in a pan on the floor under the kitchen stove would freeze, even with the stove operating at full blast. Kate and I found that Air Force surplus fleece-lined flying boots over our shoes were the answer. These we wore with warm slacks and a sleeveless shirt for winter comfort indoors. The boots had the added advantage that they polished one's shoes while being worn. It may be remarked that no one thought of moving into one of the Indian cabins, which probably could have been made much more comfortable than the wartime housing.

Even the more elaborate housing for senior members of the establishment had its problems, for the only source of heat was a coal-burning furnace and there was no proper coal to be had. DIL had managed to locate a source of "pea coal," coal in the form of nuggets about the size of an almond, which slipped swiftly through the grates if given half a chance. It was said that one slept with one ear attuned to the rustling sound in the furnace that began when the stoked fire began to fall through the grates.

If the British scientists found the management of central heating systems a problem, they could be forgiven, for the Canadians were having the same problems. Canadians, however, were better aware of the consequences of heating failures. The experience of the British physicist B.B. Kinsey and his wife, Freda, who returned from a blissful weekend in Montreal to find all the pipes burst in their house and a ball of ice protruding out of the toilet, served as a warning to the rest of the European community.

A brilliant scientist, Bernard Kinsey was already something of a legend among members of the British contingent. There was, for instance, the persistent rumour – vigorously denied by Kinsey himself – that he had been standing beside the cyclotron in Cambridge with a pair of pliers in the pocket of his new flannel "bags" when someone switched on the magnet. Obeying the inexorable laws of physics, the pliers immediately attached themselves to the magnet, ripping in the process a good part of Kinsey's "bags," which had been obtained with a gift of wartime clothing coupons from his aunts in Surrey. The students working with Kinsey at the time treasured forever afterwards his address to the perpetrator, made more memorable by a slight speech impediment. Unfortunately, no one witnessed the Kinseys' entrance to their frozen Deep River home. Bernard spoke of it to me, however, long after the trauma of the event had subsided, as "a damned, a damned, a damned nuisance."

After the war, Kate and I had the pleasure of visiting with Bernard's mother, "Solly," who lived with her sisters Hilda, Meta, and "Mrs Hippo" in a large house in Surrey. They drove about in a stately pre-war Wolseley with a speaking tube for the chauffeur. "Mrs Hippo" had taken over the driving, for – during the war – the sisters had felt that the chauffeur needed daytime rest from his duties as an air-raid warden. The sisters were kind and tender-hearted to a fault. I well remember their reaction to news that whales had been stranded on the beach at Brighton: "The poor dears!"

Staff members in Deep River who were married left their wives to cope with the problems of survival during the day. It was with some sheepishness that I would depart every day for work in a warm laboratory, leaving Kate to keep the home fires going with wood and coal. It says a great deal for the young wives, both British and Canadian – many of whom were keeping house for the first time – that they managed so well and remained cheerful and loving in the process. Those working at the plant who were unmarried lived in the Staff Hotel, where there was a central heating system and one could count on returning to a warm room in the evening.

No one had a car. The only car in the village for many months was that belonging to Mr Desbarats, the senior DIL manager. At first, transportation between the village and the plant was by an NRC station wagon, a Dodge six-cylinder truck with a wooden body built on it. This took Kowarski and his team to and from their experimental reactor.

The station wagon departed from the plant when Kowarski was ready to leave, usually after supper in the Fraser Brace cafeteria; there were usually two or three girls from the counting room together with the Canadians and New Zealanders in Kowarski's team. The trip to Deep River was often convivial, with much singing and telling of stories. "On Ilkla Moor Bar

T'Hat" was interrupted with laughter when it was discovered that one of the girls was singing "We'll Milk the Old Tom Cat." However, in those days public decorum was earnestly preserved, and the young scientist who burst into "Roll Me Over in the Clover" soon found he was singing by himself. I subsided into silence.

As the population grew, a bus service between the village and the plant was put into effect. The first buses were old school buses that had been used for students of the Commonwealth Air Training Program, and they made for cramped transportation. A weekly bus was also made available to the wives living in the village to take them shopping in Pembroke, an hour or so down the highway. Many had babies or very young children, and they had to be taken as well. It was the practice for the bus to be followed by a truck full of baby carriages and strollers. The drivers were often left babysitting in Pembroke. Pembroke, too, was the only source of wines and liquors, which became especially precious because of this. Kate tells of a tragic accident to a bottle of gin on a bus returning home. It was winter and the windows were closed, and so, to add to the misfortune, everyone came off the bus smelling of gin at the end of the trip.

Hard as early life in Deep River may have seemed to the new arrivals from Toronto and Montreal, it was a life of luxury compared to what the original inhabitants of Deep River had lived during the preceding years. Almost everyone was young, adaptable, and interested in making life as enjoyable as possible. Divisions such as that between NRC and DIL disappeared when everyone got together for concerts and parties. Even the divisions that can develop with different forms of worship seemed less important when everyone had to worship in the same hall in the Community Centre. The Catholics had a ready-built church presided over by Father McElligott, who was accessible to everyone, Catholic or not. The "Deep River Song," verses of which introduce the chapters of this book, was written

Pine Point above Deep River, looking across the river to the Quebec shore. A pen and ink drawing by Catherine de Grey in the December 1947 issue of the *Deep River Review*. Catherine has become a well-known artist in Deep River, where her paintings are prized. By special permission of the *Deep River Review*.

and composed to celebrate the second full year of life in the village of Deep River. Urbanites and an educational elite though we were, we were already coming under the spell of the Valley and, with the possible exception of the Europeans, were beginning to feel part of a historical process that had begun long before our arrival. The artists among us were painting the river in its many moods, the botanists were becoming familiar with local plants and trees, the hunters and fishermen were exploring the Quebec wilderness. The Ottawa River was becoming a part of everyone's life. Many were taking to the river in all types of watercraft and learning, sometimes at the cost of a life, to respect it. We were becoming a part of Deep River.

The song is written from the point of view of one of the original inhabitants. Whether they were in fact happier than before is, of course, open to question. Henry Adams, one of the displaced aboriginals, once said to me, "We sure miss that old river."

2

Loggers into Technicians

"Oh, I used to roll the logs for Gillies Bros.,
But I don't do that no more because
I've got a job down at the Plant with a scientific slant
Workin' on Atomic Energy."
The Deep River Song

The Ottawa has always been a highway for travel and transport. Samuel de Champlain was perhaps the first European to use it as far upstream as Deep River. In those days travel was by native canoe and it was by canoe that furs were brought from the interior to the trading posts dotted along the river. With the growth of the square timber industry, heavier and more durable boats were built: those in the timber industry had discovered that the Ottawa could be vicious. The water boundary between Ontario and Quebec was a meteorological boundary as well, given to sudden and violent storms in which fierce winds would whip down the river. The boat that evolved was called a "pointer," a heavily planked affair some thirty to fifty feet in length with a hard chine, a flat bottom, and a long, raked bow ending in a narrow point. Boats that were meant to be rowed were similarly pointed in the stern. Those using outboard motors had a square transom for mounting the motor. Even in the years after World War II, these boats could be obtained from the firm of Cockburn and Archer in Pembroke. Their pointers were painted rust-red, using the iron oxide paint known as "Tuscan Red" that is familiar on freight cars of the Canadian Pacific Railway. The Cockburn and Archer boats drew very little water. The advertisement claimed they would "float on a heavy dew."

Upstream from Deep River there used to dwell the Boom Man, who lived in the Boom House, a floating construction anchored to the Quebec shore. His task was to see that the booms guiding the logs down the Ottawa were intact and would prevent the scattering of logs along either shore.

Still further upstream were the Rapides des Joachims ("d' Swisha" in local dialect), a narrow gorge through which the entire flow of the mighty Ottawa River roared and reverberated in spray and huge standing waves. It seemed that no living thing could survive that maelstrom, but logs could be sent in twos and threes down to the pool at the foot of the rapids, where they were collected and assembled into rafts for transportation to the mills downstream or, in some cases, on down to the Lake of Two Mountains, where the brown Ottawa River flows into the green St Lawrence, and on to Quebec City. There the timber would be collected at Gilmour's Landing for use in the building of ships. The ships, loaded with white pine, would be sailed to England and there both the ships and the lumber, known as "deal," would be sold. The process created a fortune for the Gilmours, as their great house at Montrave in Fifeshire attests.

The rafts were floating camps, with a cookhouse, bunkhouses, and other facilities. They drifted with the current, guided by raftsmen with sweeps and driven with sails rigged on one or more masts mounted on the raft. At the height of the trade it was a rare day that did not see a raft manoeuvering the river past Pembroke, Arnprior, or Ottawa. At Pembroke in the late 1950s, long after the last raft had passed down the river, it was discovered that the river bottom was covered with logs that had become waterlogged on the way and had sunk to the bottom. Immersion had preserved them and an enterprise to recover timber from this treasure trove was undertaken.

In the years after World War II one could still see booms of logs going down river, but these were smaller logs destined for

the Splint Company in Pembroke, the Gillies Brothers mill at
Arnprior, or the E.B. Eddy Match Company in Pembroke and
Ottawa. The rafts were drawn by the diesel tug *Opeongo*, which
belonged to the Upper Ottawa Valley Development Company.
The name "Opeongo" has a venerable tradition in the Valley,
being the name of the first trail or road leading into the wilderness of white pine along which the early loggers traveled. There
are no more large white pines like those that made the timber
industry in the nineteenth century. The last one to be seen in
Deep River was a single tree in the foreyard of Joe Walker, the
mover. Three adults holding hands could barely encompass
the trunk near the base. Standing alone, unprotected by other
growth, it came crashing down during Hurricane Hazel in 1954.
Over two hundred annual rings were counted in the butt of
the tree. Joe sent a sixteen-foot length of it to the sawmill for
sawing into boards and found himself with a $250 bill for the
saw, which on one pass had met an iron spike, big as a man's
thumb, embedded in the heart of the log. "It tore the teeth
right off her."

————

Gillies Brothers of Arnprior had timber limits over in Quebec
across from Deep River in the forests around a 1,500-foot peak
called in the Algonquin language "Schyan." Charles Martin,
the Canadian government surveyor who made the surveys of
the plant and village properties during the war, took the opportunity to name this peak Mount Martin, and Mount Martin it
remains to the residents of Deep River to this day.

When the Ottawa River was open, logs from the Gillies' limits were drawn in booms down river by the *Opeongo*. In winter
they were carried by truck across the frozen Ottawa and down
the highway to Arnprior. The crossing was made where the
Schyan River runs out of Quebec into the Ottawa, and in
years just after the war the Gillies' Schyan Depot still stood
at the junction of the two rivers. There an ice bridge was made

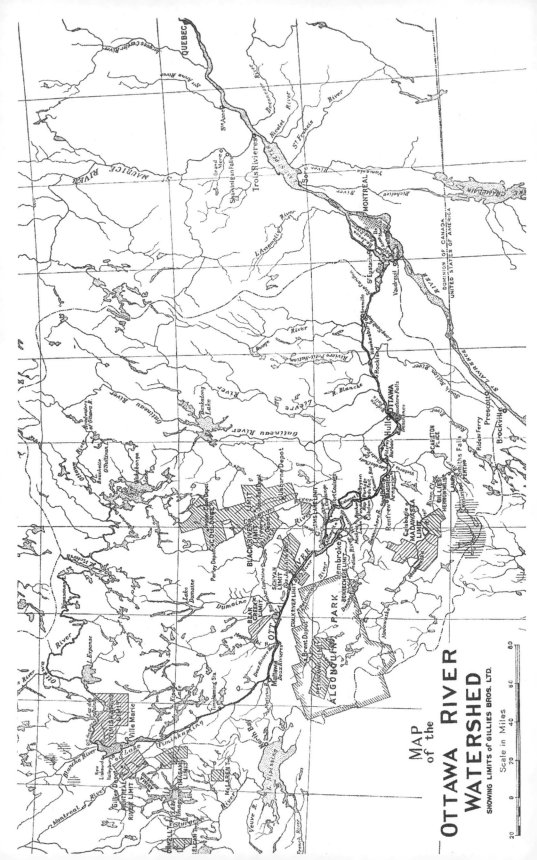

MAP
of the
OTTAWA RIVER
WATERSHED

SHOWING LIMITS of GILLIES BROS. LTD.

Scale in Miles

20   0   20   40   60   80

across the Ottawa by pumping water out onto the ice of the river in freezing conditions so that a thick trail of ice would extend from the Schyan across the Ottawa to Balmer's Bay on the Ontario shore, where a road connected with the highway. The bridge was marked by small spruce trees stuck in the snow along the way.

In the dead of winter, trucks with loads of up to five tons could negotiate the bridge with impunity. In the spring when the thaw had begun, the trip was made with considerable risk. According to Lucien Côté, the experienced trucker whose engineering skills had excited the admiration of Ian MacKay, the technique was to drive fast with both doors open. If the truck began to go, one leapt out as nimbly as possible. Lucien once told me of an incident that occurred one fine spring morning in 1946, in which his brother had the lead truck and was followed closely behind by Rabishaw, a well-known local guide and hunter. As luck would have it, the Côté truck hit a soft spot on the bridge just beyond the channel and sank, leaving a rectangular hole in the ice filled with floating logs. The driver and his companion stepped out onto the ice before the truck disappeared. Rabishaw, of course, had to stop, and then was also forced to step out, watching in horror as his brand new two-and-a-half ton Dodge truck broke through the ice and sank, leaving its load behind.

Both trucks were on the bottom in about forty feet of water. The crews attacked the problem with the dispatch and ingenuity characteristic of men accustomed to working in the bush. An A frame was constructed of tree trunks; a line of steel cable was brought out from the Ontario shore that could be reeled in by a bulldozer, and a grappling hook was fashioned that could be lowered to the sunken vehicles. The first attempt was with the Côté truck, which by chance was hooked by the front bumper. It was drawn onto the ice without a scratch, pulled to the Ontario shore, and towed to the garage in Chalk

River. By evening the truck was in running order and could be driven home.

When the crew assembled next morning they were surprised to find Rabishaw with an enormously long probe made of lathes lashed together. He was full of precautions about how the grappling hook should be placed; his truck was new and he wanted the boys to be careful with it. He probed and lowered the grappling hook. When he was finally satisfied with the placement he signaled for the pull. There was momentary resistance; then the cable came up slack with the door of the truck attached to the hook. Poor Rabishaw, still convinced that he could control the situation, tried again. This time there was resistance all the way. The truck appeared with the grappling hook embedded in the roof of the cab, which ripped apart just as the truck surfaced and allowed the truck to sink once more into the depths. Rabishaw, completely shattered by this outcome, allowed the others to salvage the truck as best they could. They did it upon the next try.

It was characteristic of Valley men that this story was always greeted with raucous laughter at the expense of Rabishaw. Everyone was well acquainted with misfortune and hardship; the only appropriate reaction was to laugh at it.

·————·

Balmer's Bay (it is "Balmer" on the map) is a shallow bay two or three miles down river from Deep River and was the location of one of the very few farms, the Robert farm, on the Ontario shore. In the days when the wood-burning steamer *Oiseau* plied the river between Pembroke and the Rapides des Joachims, it was a point of call for passengers and fuel. Mrs Robert was a fine figure of a woman, nearly six feet tall and generously proportioned. Mr David Gillies recalled an incident in 1937 when, as a passenger on the *Oiseau*, he witnessed the loading of eleven cords of wood onto the steamer by Mrs Robert and her husband. She told Mr Gillies afterwards, "I was tired, but he was DEAD!"

Poor Robert was indeed ailing, and he died shortly thereafter. She remarried, and was Mrs Adeline Mercereau when the new people began coming to Deep River. It was as Mrs Mercereau that she became something of a thorn in the side of DIL. The Project had to negotiate the purchase of property impinging on her farm and Mrs Mercereau was not one to accept meekly the fact that the land was needed by the Government of Canada. She had, after all, in her time been a visitor to the World's Fair in Chicago and had brought her personal complaints and suggestions to the fair's general manager, who had been most accommodating, and she had had her picture taken with him for the *Chicago Tribune* on that occasion. She was also well known to Father McElligott, who advised DIL to proceed softly. Even after the negotiation was accomplished, she complained bitterly to Kate and me that the fence that DIL put up would fall over "if a rabbit lean't on it."

The fence was pretty flimsy. This was perhaps why, many years later when the village had become well established, there was an invasion in the dead of night by a herd of cattle from the Mercereau farm. Those who had coaxed vegetable gardens out of the sandy soil spent the night in sleepless vigilance. Word got around next day that one of the village doctors, a rather reserved individual, had been seen in his pajamas and bare feet chasing a steer out of his backyard.

————

As the Project matured in the years after the war, many of the men who had logged or worked in the bush became employed as riggers and fitters, carpenters and outdoor workers, positions requiring mechanical skills, if not much education. Some, by training, became highly skilled operators of equipment for the remote handling of radioactive material, for it was the handling of radioactive material that differentiated the plant from most other industrial ventures then known in Canada.

Knowledge of radioactivity goes back only to the dawn of the twentieth century, although radioactivity has always been a feature of life on Earth. It was Marie Sklodowska Curie with her husband, Pierre, who in Paris first isolated pure radium from uranium ore and demonstrated that it was the source of the mysterious rays emanating from the ore. It was known that these rays would darken photographic plates even when the plates were kept completely wrapped in heavy black paper. The Curies and others soon showed that the rays could be separated into three kinds and identified them with the Greek letters alpha, beta, and gamma. The alpha and beta rays were relatively easily stopped. It was clear that the alphas never would have got through the black paper. Enough thicknesses of paper would have stopped the betas, too, but the gammas could not be attenuated except by thick sheets of lead, one of the densest metals known.

This kind of penetrating radiation had been seen before. Wilhelm Roentgen had developed toward the end of the nineteenth century a device for generating what we now call X-rays, radiation that would penetrate the human hand and show on a photographic plate the bone structure of the palm and fingers. The higher the voltage he applied to his X-ray tube, the more penetrating the X-rays became and the thicker and heavier the material required to absorb them. The penetration of the gamma rays of the radium isolated by the Curies corresponded to voltages higher than ever produced by electric equipment. Other than this much higher energy, the gamma rays appeared to be much like X-rays.

Marie Curie went on to isolate other pure elements from ores showing penetrating radiations. The element "polonium" she named after her motherland, Poland. She called this class of substances "*radioactif*." Radioactivity therefore refers to the class

Two excerpts from "Plutonium Pete: A Story in Extracts From the Press" by Nicholas Miller, published in the October 1946 edition of the *Deep River Review*.

———————.

Time, July 22, 1958

RADIANT PERCEPTION

Hottest news of the week in both physical and biological sciences was the report of Rome University's handsome, dark-skinned Dr Donizetti, 38, that his chimpanzee Pete had been established as a detector of nuclear radiation. Colleagues at the Smithsonian Institute watched in stunned silence July 15th as the sensitive simian infallibly pointed to the one of a number of identical lead containers which contained 200 milligrams of radium. Applause resounded at each performance, in which the ape joined lustily.

———————.

Los Angeles Examiner, August 2, 1958

APE AN ACE WITH ACTIVITIES
SIMIAN A SCIENTIFIC SIZZLER, SAY SAVANTS

OAK RIDGE, Tenn., Aug. 1 (AP) – Dr Donizetti's simian wizard, now christened "Plutonium Pete" for his fascination for the fissile element, created a sensation in the "hot" chemistry laboratories here today, when he went wild with excitement after identifying correctly a number of beakers and flasks containing radioactive solutions.

WASHINGTON, D.C., Aug. 1 (AP) – The allegiance of Dr Donizetti's monkey marvel, Pete, has been receiving considerable attention here today. It is reported that the F.B.I.

have found considerable difficulty in finding a precedent for investigating the allegiance and nationality of a non-human visitor. Meantime Sen. Bilgo (D.,Miss) is reported to have told friends that the ape is "nothing but a damned Communist" and that "apes and niggers should be excluded from atom know-how."

Pete's fan-mail, now running in excess of 2000 daily, is being handled by a company of the Army Intelligence. Numerous proposals of marriage are reported to be included.

———————

My sketch of Plutonium Pete as an illustration for the above article shows the Simian Savant as a member of the Chalk River Project. This is a typical "film badge" worn by all scientists and workers in the project. It was relinquished at the gatehouse upon leaving in the evening and picked up in the morning upon arrival. Behind the photograph was a dental film whose darkening by penetrating radiation was carefully monitored every week. Of the hundreds of thousands of such films monitored over the years, very few – perhaps ten or twenty – showed enough darkening to warrant a follow-up investigation.

of materials that emit spontaneously alpha, beta, or gamma radiation, or combinations of all three. These radiations are produced from processes in the material itself, originating in the atoms.

————

The discovery of X-rays led, as we know, to their widespread use in medical diagnostics, and there are few orthopedic, dental, and other treatments today that do not use X-rays as a diagnostic tool. Radium, when it was discovered, was at first similarly accepted by professionals and the public as a wonder capable of great things, although it was not exactly clear what it did. Elaborate and luxurious spas were built around springs reputed to have appreciable concentrations of radium in the water, and for a considerable sum guests were encouraged to take a course of treatments involving baths and daily drinks of the elixir. Applications were also found where radium could be used to produce numerals that glowed in the dark, and the manufacture of radium dials for watches became an established process.

More to the point was the use of the radiations from radium to treat tumours and cancers. This last development led to the discovery that penetrating radiation could have harmful effects upon healthy human tissue, producing microscopic lesions that could lead to cancer. Evidence began to accumulate of harmful effects of penetrating radiations. Miners in the uranium mines in Joachimstahl in Czechoslovakia, where mining had been in progress for more than a hundred years before the discovery of radium, developed lung cancer almost as an occupational disease. The women who painted watch dials with luminous paint used to lick their brushes to a fine point and many developed cancer of the lip and tongue. Even X-rays were shown to be harmful when used in excess. Repeated demonstrations of the bone structure of the hand could lead to severe skin cancer. Marie Curie herself became a victim of her discovery and died from what is believed to have been overexposure to penetrating radiation.

These negative aspects of penetrating radiation took a long time to reach the general public. Even as late as World War II, major shoe stores in Canada and the United States featured a device that allowed the buyer to examine the fit of the shoe by looking into an X-ray machine generating radiation of sufficient penetration to pass through both shoe and foot and project the resulting image on a fluorescent screen. The buyer viewing the image received an appreciable exposure to the X-rays, but as he or she probably did not buy more than one or two pairs of shoes a year, the danger of overexposure was not great. However, a second viewer allowed the sales clerk to examine the fit as well, and it was the clerk who, working all day with the device, was in danger. It is not known to what extent the clerks may have suffered from this occupational hazard, but the awareness of danger among professionals working in the field led to a Canadian government ban on these machines in 1946.

Today there is widespread appreciation of the hazards posed by penetrating radiation of any kind. The heavy, lead-filled apron fitted to the patient receiving a dental X-ray is only one example of the precautions that have become routine. At the Chalk River Project the task of insuring the protection of workers against overexposure to radiation fell to the Health Radiation Branch operated by DIL. These people had the double task of educating plant personnel as well as insuring that techniques and processes were safe, for in the early days of the Project the workers shared the ignorance that was typical of the general public. The scientists often felt that the plant regulations were a hindrance to their work, and some felt that they knew as much or more about the problems of safety as the people in the Health Radiation Branch. In this there was some truth, for it was up to the scientists to develop the instruments for the detection and measurement of radiation. It is fair to say that, if penetrating radiation represents the cost of using the power in the atom, its properties make it possible to construct instruments of such sensitivity that levels of radiation far below permissible levels are easily detected and measured.

Work on the construction of these instruments was one of the first tasks undertaken by the Project while it was still situated in the University of Montreal, before the move to Chalk River. The earliest hand-held device was a shoebox-sized sheet steel box, heavy with batteries, called a "Lily." Developed by young, unmarried engineers and technicians, it had been named in honour of Lily St Cyr, a stripper who was then the toast of Montreal. The next version, a considerable improvement in weight and sensitivity, was called the "Super-Lily," and went through several models. With improved knowledge of radiation properties and detection methods, together with the miniaturization of components characteristic of modern electronics, small instruments of great sensitivity are commonly used today.

Much research has also gone into determining what level of radiation can be considered permissible from the standpoint of human health. Here one enters an arena of conflicting views. Those fundamentally opposed to the use of atomic energy argue that any level of radiation is deleterious to human health. On the other hand, all forms of life on Earth have been exposed to penetrating radiation from natural sources since time immemorial.

It is probably true that some scientists in the early days of the Project, particularly those who had worked in the field before coming to Chalk River, were exposed to levels of radiation above those that would be permitted today. It must also be said that some of those who were known to have been careless have lived to a ripe old age without showing effects of exposure. This does not excuse carelessness, and current precautions against overexposure are manifold and rigorously enforced.

————.

The early days of the Chalk River Project were a time of improvisation and accommodation. Buildings were for the most part still under construction, the most important of which, Building 100, was to house NRX, the National Research Council Experimental Reactor. Construction on this was practically complete by the end of the war, but the reactor start-up was delayed for a further two years owing to minor problems. The building housing Kowarski's low power reactor experiment was among the first to be finished.

This was a barn-sized structure containing a large tank of "heavy water," needed for the nuclear reactor. Popular rumour had it that the Ottawa River site had been chosen because heavy water could be obtained at great depths near the bottom of the river. This was fantasy. All water contains a minute fraction of heavy water, as was first discovered by Prof. H.C. Urey of Columbia University, and pure heavy water can be obtained only by costly extraction from vast quantities of ordinary water. The heavy water so extracted is very expensive; in 1945 it cost about $250 per litre in 1945 dollars. Bill Prosser, of Chalk River Operations staff, recalls that the Project bureaucrats and cost accountants at first proposed a regulation that would send to prison any person disposing of heavy water. A scientist pointed out that anyone who flushed a toilet would be liable for imprisonment, and the idea was dropped.

In 1939 Lew Kowarski, working at the Collége de France in Paris, had determined that this scarce substance would be extremely important to the success of the French attempt to develop energy from the atom. The only source accessible at that time was an extraction plant in Norway. Kowarski obtained permission from the French government to buy the plant's entire stock, about 180 litres. When the Germans invaded France, Frédéric Joliot, the director of the laboratory, determined that the stock should not fall into German hands.

Arrangements were made to transport Kowarski and his heavy water on roads choked with refugees to the coast at Bordeaux and thence by ship to England and to the Cavendish Laboratory in Cambridge so that his work might continue. With the formation of the British atomic energy project, the decision was made in 1942 to transfer all work in this field to the Montreal Laboratory in Canada, out of range of German bombers. Kowarski and his precious heavy water therefore made a further voyage across the Atlantic.

————

In a fitting conclusion to this monumental pilgrimage to safety, Kowarski led his team of Canadians and New Zealanders at Chalk River to the successful completion of his experiment. A reactor was constructed of uranium and heavy water in which a sustained reaction based on the energy in the atom could be achieved. The acronym for this device was ZEEP, the Zero Energy Experimental Pile, the designation "Pile" being derived from the French *pile*, meaning a battery, or a repetitive assembly of energy generating units. The term soon fell into disuse, quite simply because it was a poor description of the process by which energy was being generated.

In September 1945, therefore, the world's first self-sustaining atomic reactor outside of the United States was brought into being at the Chalk River Project. A national historic plaque raised on the hillside above the ZEEP building notes the fact. ZEEP's success crowned years of effort in France, England, and Canada, and it made Canada a major player in the newly opening field of atomic energy. For those who regard this bit of history with apprehension it would perhaps be significant to note that someone had crowned one of ZEEP's instrument panels with the grisly skull and horns of a cow, found at the plant in a former pasture.

ZEEP was to serve for many years as a low power test reactor for nuclear fuel and lattice arrangements. Kowarski returned to France soon after the success of ZEEP to become a major figure in the French atomic energy commission, le Commissariat pour l'Energie Atomique. He returned to Chalk River only once, for a brief visit. I chatted with him in his old age many years later at a meeting of the American Physical Society in Boston, and he recalled with a chuckle the days spent "*dans un pays sauvage.*"

————

From 1946 and onward the settlement at Deep River began to burgeon with activities. Never before in the history of Canada had such a large community of highly skilled and educated young people and their families been situated in isolation in what was almost virgin wilderness. In the absence of organized entertainment the community fell to and formed clubs of all kinds. Within a period of eighteen months Deep River could boast of at least sixty clubs, ranging from chess to cross-country and downhill skiing.

The Mount Martin Ski Club soon opened trails through the bush on the Ontario shore. The more adventurous could ski across the river into the wilderness of Quebec; the better skiers could climb Mount Martin and ski back down. This was risky in the extreme, for the trail was not maintained and one never knew what one might run into. Ed de Grey once came flying down into a family of wolves and scattered them in every direction. Had he fallen and been hurt, the story might have become grim.

Summer brought with it a new range of activities, and the community took to the Ottawa River in all sorts of craft. The Deep River Yacht Club banded together and built during the winter a series of one-class boats suitable for racing. These were "Y-flyers," a type of inland water, centre-board scow, very fast, with Marconi-rigged sails and a crew of two. Competition was keen. Kate and I owned Y-107. In one race in high winds I fell overboard. Kate's first reaction was to grab and secure the sheet I had released so as not to lose our position in the race. (I could swim and I thoroughly approved of her sense of priorities.) The fleet eventually grew to a dozen or more boats and produced some champion sailors. The Yacht Club went on to great things and today represents one of the most important sailing organizations in eastern Ontario. Few, if any, could boast more magnificent waters.

One usually finds in any community with a concentration of English people that, sooner or later, a theatre or drama group is formed, and Deep River proved to be no exception. The Drama Club was soon thriving, and its productions verged on the professional. The plays were enthusiastically received by the community and the club went from strength to strength, eventually winning prizes in drama festivals throughout the province.

It was not long before those with editorial pretensions began to publish a periodical, the *Deep River Review,* an effort generously supported by local advertisers. The quality of writing was good; one contributor, Freda Kinsey, went on to publish in the *New Yorker*, and autobiographical articles by Sir John Cockcroft made certain issues of the magazine collector's items. As might have been predicted, however, the magazine had little appeal for its general readership, being as it was a vehicle for the literary fancies of its erudite contributors and for a somewhat convoluted sense of humour. Despite cartoons and the occasional popular article, advertisers withdrew their support one by one, and publication ceased after four quarterly issues.

————

Few of the scientific personnel would have had time to write on subjects outside their fields of specialization, particularly as the pace of research and development at Chalk River quickened. It became the rule, rather than the exception, to work in the evening as well as during the day. This meant overtime at the Project, or at least evenings reading and writing at home, for the scientists were expected to keep up with reading in their chosen field on their own time. This was often difficult when one had a young family. As one young physicist, John Ferguson, was heard to sigh, "I'll bet Sir Isaac Newton never had to come home to crying children!"

The scientists were also expected to maintain their competence and to publish original work. This was a full-time job in every sense. For this they were given the security of a modest salary and were rented accommodation from the stock of housing maintained by the Project. Their personal well-being and the well-being of their families were in this way limited to what was available. The non-professionals, the hourly rate workers and administrators, had no such constraints. Once at home, their time was their own. Many of the more competent used this time to build homes that were either sold or rented for a considerable profit. Some became well-to-do builders and developers and much of the peripheral development of Deep River came about as a result of their activities. The professionals thus often found themselves at a financial disadvantage vis-à-vis their non-professional colleagues in Deep River and might be pardoned for envying, as some did, the lot of their fellow-scientists in Russia, who were being supported by the state as a privileged elite. Despite such problems most scientists and engineers in Deep River managed to live full and rewarding lives. Many took part in such demanding activities as plays and musicals and in the great range of activities offered by the many clubs.

Special occasions saw the village come together for mass celebrations, the Bean Supper at Father McElligott's church, Christmas parades, and, of course, concerts and plays. Perhaps most memorable were the festivities of 2 June 1953, on the occa-

sion of the coronation of Queen Elizabeth II. The committee
in charge came up with the idea that an ox should be publicly
roasted to provide a feast for the celebration. The machine shop
at the plant provided a sturdy spit to hold the weight of the ani-
mal and a site was chosen on the waterfront accessible to electric power, so that the spit could be rotated by an electric motor.
A firepit was dug and a good supply of firewood brought to
the site. It had been discovered that a whole ox, cleaned and
butchered, was not to be had for love nor money, so the committee had to content itself with two complete sides of beef,
wired together around the spit. Volunteers were organized to
keep the fire going for the hours and hours needed to cook the
beef, and thirty or forty thermocouples were inserted into the
meat to monitor temperatures throughout. Charlie Miller, a
rather racy young bachelor who advertised himself as an example of how easy it was to obtain a Ph.D. in physics at McGill
University (he was a very good physicist), entered wholeheart-
edly into the festivities. Dressed in a frowsy blond wig and not
much else, he represented an "early Saxon."

The fire was lit with great fanfare on the evening of 1 June
and was kept going throughout the night by volunteers in two-
hour shifts and into the following afternoon, when the village
was invited to partake of "oxburgers" at fifty cents apiece. The
community responded, but, despite strong feelings of loyalty to
the new Queen, could not stomach the "oxburgers." The beef,
after all the preparation, was by no means cooked through. The
dogs of the village had a field day, and knowing the Queen's
fondness for animals, that is perhaps the way she would have
had it.

———————

We were all young in those days. The average age of Deep
River inhabitants was around thirty years. There were many
young children, most of whom had never seen anyone with

grey or white hair or a full beard. Someone's bearded naval uncle came up for a weekend early in the history of the village. He made a profound impression on the children: "Mom, Jesus Christ is skiing on the dump hill!" "I saw Jesus shopping at the A and P."

It was the dawn of high fidelity electronic sound reproduction, and many who had access to electronic components in the laboratories used to build amplifiers for what was known as "the Chinese government." That is, they were doing "government" work on their lunch hours and in overtime. This "justified" the use of government components and equipment. Dr Hugh Carmichael, the branch head of Technical Physics Branch, looked with tolerance on these activities for, as he said, the individuals doing this were learning a good deal of electronics in the process. Furthermore, isolated as we were from large commercial centres, the plant was the only ready source of the required materials.

Deep River was said to have the largest concentration of Ph.D.s in Canada, and the degree of excellence shown in the many leisure activities may have been due to the presence of so many "achievers." Apparently the drive for excellence in professional life carried over into free time. The amplifiers built were often very fine and reproduced faithfully every tick and scratch on the records that were then available. The recordings became the limiting factor in the music produced. Fortunately, the demand for high fidelity, low noise recordings began to be felt in the market. Similarly, the work done in the Woodworking Club was often fine enough to pass muster in the most demanding markets. Racing yachts were built by members of the Yacht Club with great precision and care; the weight of every screw and fitting was counted. The same Hugh Carmichael became a champion sailor who eventually built a sail-loft onto his house and cut and sewed his own sails. His colleague, John Steljes, a brilliant physics technician and a

trained organist, built at home an early electronic organ, repro-
ducing electronically the quality of sound produced by famous
organs of Europe and America. This was no project for "the
Chinese government" and was completed before the advent of
transistors, a feat in itself. John's daughter Cynthia has carried
on the musical tradition of the family as oboist in the famous
"Quartetto Gelato."

A feature of all this activity was that many professionals, scientists as well as engineers, became proficient in a wide range
of trades of all kinds. The services taken for granted in urban
communities were, at least in the early years, almost non-existent. If something had to be done, one did it oneself. Heads
of families were called upon to perform tasks ranging from
carpentry, plumbing repairs, and electrical wiring to adjusting
furnaces and the repair of appliances. If anything went wrong,
the first step was to determine how the thing worked, then to
correct the fault. Homemade household gadgets of all kinds
flourished in this environment. Bill Grummitt, a chemist distinguished for his work in measuring trace amounts of radioactivity in the environment, was a dedicated gardener as well as
a champion sailor. He had his garden instrumented and wired
so that it rang an alarm by his bed if there was a danger of frost.

One might say that in many respects Deep River men made
ideal husbands. Advanced degrees in education and outstanding technical competence do not protect against upheavals of
emotion, however, and Deep River, like any other Canadian
community, had its share of marital crises and other human
woes. These may have appeared unusually intense to the inhabitants of the village since they did not have the anonymity of
events in an urban community, but it seems doubtful that they
were exceptional in any way.

The friendly contacts made in the many village clubs and
activities carried over into the working lives of men and women
in the Project, and for the scientists and engineers, at least,

often led to an interdisciplinary approach to the solution of problems. The network of friendships contributed to an information network within the Project that had a consolidating and unifying effect. Whether senior management was aware of the process and encouraged it is a matter for speculation. It certainly existed and helped to make Chalk River the successful research and development centre that it became.

3

Wartime Secrecy

"Well, the boys down at the plant, they made me swear
That I'd never tell you what goes on down there.
But shovelin' sand for sixty cents is just the same inside a fence,
Workin' on Atomic Energy!"
                                        The Deep River Song

The Rideau River, an Ontario tributary of the Ottawa, winds through the city of Ottawa on its way to the Rideau Falls, where it tumbles over a short cliff into the Ottawa, forming the curtain of water that gives the Rideau its name. On its way, the Rideau laps at the back door of the embassy of the former Union of Soviet Socialist Republics, providing – one can imagine – a convenient avenue for clandestine comings and goings to and from that squat, fortress-like building. The Russians were our allies for most of the Second World War, but for a number of reasons – and mainly at the insistence of the United States – they were excluded from sharing in the results of the work being done on atomic energy. The Americans were able to boast that the nuclear weapons released on Hiroshima and Nagasaki were the best-kept secret of the war. The "atomic bombs," as they were called, took the world by surprise. They were not, as it turned out, a complete surprise to the Russians.

Secrecy had been the watchword of the U.S. atomic energy project all during the war and for many years after. Under the direction of U.S. Army engineer Gen. Leslie R. Groves, the U.S. project was controlled at every step and in every department by security officers who went to great lengths to insure secrecy. These officers accompanied scientists and officials even when traveling between organizations within the project, to insure that no information not directly related to the visit was released. Well-known scientists traveled under false names; laboratories doing related work, even those in universities, were kept under lock and key. Scientists and engineers working at the Los Alamos Laboratory were interned in that remote site for the duration of the war and for several months after the capitulation of Japan. This tight security led inevitably to confusion and duplication of work even in the years following World War II. Americans used to enjoy visiting Chalk River during that period because – among other things – they could find out what was going on in other laboratories in the States.

All this was in direct antithesis to what had been the spirit of international scientific research. Atomic research had been conducted by an international community of physicists, chemists, and mathematicians right up to the early years of the war. Most of the information required for the development of the atomic bomb was published in 1940, when Prof. James Stranathan of the United States brought out his textbook *The Particles of Modern Physics* and summarized for all to see the scientific developments basic to exploiting atomic energy. Scientists were working in the field in all the major laboratories in Europe, and papers with new results and new ideas were being submitted for publication almost daily.

The breakthrough had come at the end of 1938 in the laboratory of Prof. Otto Hahn of the University of Berlin, working with long-time associates Dr Lise Meitner and Dr Fritz Strassmann. Hahn and Strassmann were able to demonstrate conclusively that when uranium was subjected to radiation from a mixed source of radium and beryllium, new elements were formed that were roughly half the mass of uranium. Dr Meitner, meanwhile, had been labouring under the stigma of being "non-Aryan" in Hitler's Third Reich, and circumstances had forced her to leave Germany for Sweden during the preceding month. Hahn and Strassmann could not explain what they had demonstrated and what would later be correctly interpreted by others. Their achievement tends to get lost in the thunderous aftermath of their discovery. The source of radiation was so weak and the amounts of material affected by the radiation so small that it was only by the most sensitive radio-chemical techniques that the identification of the products was made.

In Copenhagen, in an elegant physics laboratory on the grounds of (and funded by) the famous Carlsberg Brewery, Dr Meitner's nephew Otto Frisch, a talented musician and theoretical physicist, was working as a colleague of the great Danish physicist and theoretician Niels Bohr. Lise Meitner's old chief, Otto Hahn – in a demonstration of how little Hitler's dogma meant to many Germans – kept her in touch with all that was happening in the Berlin laboratory. During the 1938 Christmas holidays, Meitner related to her nephew, who was visiting in Sweden, what had been discovered in Berlin. Frisch saw immediately the implications of the discovery: the effect of irradiation with the radium-beryllium source had been to cause atoms of uranium to split roughly into two halves. Once back in Copenhagen, Frisch wasted no time in setting up the simple apparatus needed to confirm this idea, and on 12 January 1939, aunt and nephew sent a letter to the journal *Nature* propounding their explanation of the phenomenon and describing the experimental confirmation. Frisch christened the atom-splitting process "fissioning" of uranium. His demonstration showed that the fission process released enormous amounts of energy, though on a microscopic scale.

It is a comment on the chemical and physical approaches to the problem that Frisch was able to demonstrate fission with quite simple apparatus. The minute quantities of fission products collected meant that the chemistry had to be done with great precision and care, whereas the physical apparatus of the day was quite capable of detecting single atomic events.

The radium-beryllium source used in these experiments produced, in addition to alpha, beta, and gamma radiation from the radium, particles of a kind that had been identified only a few years before by James Chadwick (later Sir James) at Cambridge. This radiation, like alpha and beta radiation, is composed of particles. They are called "neutrons" since, unlike alpha or beta particles, they are electrically neutral. It was neutrons emitted by the beryllium irradiated with alpha particles from the radium in the mixed source that had caused the splitting or "fissioning" of uranium.

Neutrons are central to nuclear fission and therefore central to any story of the development of atomic energy. They play a major role in this story of Canada's first steps into the nuclear age.

————

Meitner and Frisch had speculated on the possibility that the fission of uranium might be accompanied by the emission of further neutrons. Lew Kowarski and Hans von Halban, working with Frédéric Joliot at the Collége de France in Paris, showed a few weeks later that, yes indeed, the fission was accompanied by the emission of several neutrons. The stage was thus set for a self-sustaining process. If one or more of these neutrons induced further fission, the process could go on indefinitely, or at least until terminated by an explosion or by some other means. An explosion, even of a small amount of fissionable material, would be volcanic in effect – something never before caused by the human hand.

There were, of course, limitations. Many other materials capture neutrons and thus can rob neutrons from the fission process: any self-sustaining fission reaction would have to be contained in vessels made of materials that did not capture too many neutrons. On the other hand, highly neutron-absorptive materials, such as the element boron, could be used to control or even "douse" the self-sustaining fission process.

———.

Bohr was about to leave Copenhagen for a meeting of the American Physical Society in New York when the Meitner-Frisch letter was sent to *Nature*. He took with him the news from Berlin together with Meitner's and Frisch's explanation of what had happened. He reported all this to his former student, J.A. Wheeler, and to physicists and chemists attending the Physical Society meeting, many of whom did not wait for the end of the meeting to rush back to their laboratories to confirm the discovery. One can imagine the excitement when Bohr, speaking in his soft voice, almost inaudible to a large audience, explained in his heavily accented English, with its rising and falling Danish intonation, the details of Hahn's and Strassmann's discovery and its implications for the future.

———.

Those who dreaded the implications the most were the many European scientists who had fled Europe in fear of Nazi domination. There were many Jews among them, like James Franck, who were already familiar with Nazi persecution. Leo Szilard, a Hungarian chemist, took an initiative many of the expatriate Europeans felt was necessary. He wrote to Albert Einstein, himself now a refugee, asking him to warn President Roosevelt as to what these discoveries might mean in the hands of Adolf Hitler. If Hitler could build an atomic weapon based on the fissioning of uranium, he would dominate Europe and possibly the world. The letter Einstein wrote is a landmark in history.

It is remarkable that a man with the stature of Roosevelt was president of the United States at that critical moment. Einstein's letter to Roosevelt was delivered by Alexander Sachs, a well-known financier and friend of the president. Roosevelt's immediate response was to set in motion events that led to the formation of a highly secretive project to develop the military use of atomic energy. According to that project's official history, American-born scientists at the time were so unaccustomed to the idea of using their science for military purposes that they had no idea how to proceed. The initiative was taken by expatriate Europeans, Leo Szilard, Eugene Wigner, Edward Teller, and others, who were instrumental in keeping up pressure on the president's military advisers to proceed with the organization necessary to create an atomic weapon. At the same time it was mentioned that useful atomic power could also be an outcome of the project.

The first allocation of funds was an amount of $6,000, transferred in the autumn of 1939 from the U.S. Army and U.S. Navy to buy uranium and graphite for the project. By the end of World War II, expenditures had totalled over $2 billion, several large research, development, and production centres had been established, and a significant proportion of the country's scientific manpower from both industry and the universities had been engaged. This vast effort culminated in the atomic bombs detonated at Hiroshima and Nagasaki. It was known as the "Manhattan Project."

Roosevelt was no anglophile. He held no brief for officers of his own State Department, who, he felt, too often aped the ways of their counterparts in the British Foreign Office. (Some of them did.) But in 1939 he saw the international situation as clearly as did Winston Churchill, who was then poised to enter his greatest hour. Roosevelt was therefore prepared to assist Britain in any way he could, short of going to war, but he had to tread softly to placate his strong isolationist constituencies. Thanks to this attitude, there was early cooperation in atomic energy between Britain and the United States, a cooperation that led eventually to the formation of the international project in Montreal.

With the establishment of the Manhattan Project and the international project in Montreal, scientific research in atomic energy was hidden behind a thick veil of secrecy that was not relaxed until a decade after the war. Even today, some developments are concealed from the eyes of the world.

———————

Secrecy of the Montreal project was a prime consideration, both in Montreal and at the Chalk River site. The Royal Canadian Mounted Police guarded the entrance to "D" wing of the University of Montreal, where the project was located; all Canadians involved in the project had to have clearance from the RCMP. Britons were signatories to the Official Secrets Act, and the French were accepted in good faith as Free French opponents of the Vichy government and enemies of the Third Reich. Being Canada, however, security was enforced in a rather gentle way, at least to the public eye, in comparison to methods employed in the United States. The avuncular RCMP corporal at the entrance to the laboratories at the University of Montreal got to know everyone personally, but let himself be hoodwinked from time to time by young scientists spiriting containers of lab alcohol and other useful items out of the laboratory. The gates at the Chalk River Project were protected by middle-aged guards armed with unloaded shotguns, whereas the Oak Ridge Laboratories in Tennessee had manned machine-gun emplacements on either side of the entrance.

Bill Prosser, a colleague of mine at Chalk River, relates that on a mission to Fernald, Ohio, where secret work was being done for the Chalk River Project, he was given a desk in the general office. He was working quietly when he noticed a hush descend over the office. Looking up, he saw two young men enter, the first with a briefcase in one hand and a drawn pistol in the other; the second had a pistol in each hand. They advanced slowly, looking around suspiciously. The man with the briefcase then holstered his gun and opened the case and emptied the contents of the first wastebasket into it. This was repeated at each desk. The man with the briefcase (which was chained to his wrist) closed the case and locked it. The men then left. "I asked what was going on, and was told that these men were getting rid of any secret material which might have gone into the wastebaskets. Also that they were so trigger happy that the staff were afraid to move during the process for fear of getting shot!"

There was only one occasion when bullets whistled and whined over the plant at Chalk River. Local deer hunters had decided that the extensive fence around the plant would be ideal for driving deer. So one November morning shots rang out from the ridge behind the plant and stray bullets zinged over Building 100, which housed the NRX reactor. The plant guards deployed in force under the direction of their captain, Peter McConnachie, and apprehended the culprits, who were suitably chastised and fined. My friend Lucien Côté was, I am sorry to say, among them. Knowing him as I did, I fear that he was the organizer of the hunt.

———————

Project security during the war extended to the village of Deep River, and no one was admitted without a pass, which was examined by the guards at the gate. Ruth Hatfield once took her latest infant in his perambulator for a stroll outside the gate. To her dismay, she found she had forgotten her pass. The guard apparently knew her husband, Gordie Hatfield, a senior DIL manager, for he let Ruth through the gate, saying that the baby looked so much like Gordie that he couldn't be anyone else's child.

The RCMP officer charged with reviewing the secrecy provisions in the village of Deep River stated that it was literally impossible to maintain the secrecy of any subject there. As an instance, it was reported that at one of the afternoon parties some village wives somehow got onto the topic of male circumcision, and each revealed whether her husband was circumcised or not. In no time it was general knowledge in the village as to who was circumcised and who wasn't. This became part of the information one carried about these colleagues and acquaintances. Whether this situation extended to more serious state secrets is open to question. There was never known to be a major breach of security in the history of the village, though questions were later raised about U.K. physicist Bruno Pontecorvo, who lived in Deep River during the early days.

The United States maintained a liaison office in the Canadian project from the time the two countries agreed to collaborate in the development of atomic energy. Its official function was to facilitate the exchange of information. This was certainly done, but it also seems likely that the main idea was to keep an eye on what was going on in Canada. George Weil was the U.S. liaison officer in the early days of the project at Chalk River. He was distinguished by his ability to mix martini cocktails of unusual power and efficacy. He may, however, have had reservations about Canadian security, for the U.S. habitually dragged its feet in the matter of exchanges of scientific information. There were, of course, several reasons for this. Hans von Halban, who had been chosen to head the project in Montreal, had been suspected of having communist sympathies. After all, Frédéric Joliot, his chief in Paris, made no secret of the fact that he was left-leaning. Halban's replacement by Dr Cockcroft had eased somewhat this impasse. Then again, the Americans feared that the Europeans in the Canadian project might be vulnerable to pressure because of relatives left behind in a Nazi-controlled Europe.

————

The discovery in time of real breaches in security showed that concerns had been well founded. The first indication of trouble was in the Montreal Laboratory, where physicists and chemists were in the process of establishing the chemistry of a new element, plutonium, with a total of nineteen milligrams of the material obtained from the Manhattan Project. This amount could, literally, be carried on the head of a pin. Chemical tests were conducted under binocular microscopes, using techniques of the most exquisite sensitivity. Under the direction of Prof. Jules Guéron, one of the Free French scientists, a complete science of micro-chemistry had been developed for the study. Then one morning it was discovered that only eight milligrams of the plutonium could be accounted for: eleven milligrams had apparently been misplaced or spilled. The laboratory was in a pandemonium. A.G. "Alphie" Maddock, who was later to establish a radiochemistry laboratory at Cambridge, was found sawing off part of the lab bench to be dissolved in acid and extracted for the lost plutonium. Although every possibility was examined, the missing plutonium could not be found. Guéron had to admit ruefully to the director, Dr Cockcroft, that "We are very poor chemists."

The agents behind this and other possible losses to the project were not uncovered, at least to the public, until a cipher clerk in the Russian embassy, Igor Gouzenko, defected, bearing undeniable proof of an extensive Russian spy ring involving several Canadians in positions of responsibility as well as two English workers in the Montreal project. They were Alan Nunn May, a physicist, whom I remember as a man of medium height with a blank face bearing a small moustache, and Norman Veall, a churlish, black-haired little technician who looked sourly upon the world while producing elegant and sensitive instruments for the detection and measurement of radiation. The information provided by Gouzenko was greeted with shocked disbelief. Even the Mounties could not be convinced of it, though the documents were undeniably authentic. Gouzenko, at considerable danger to himself and his family in Ottawa, persisted until the Canadian government was finally persuaded of the facts of the case. Mackenzie King, the prime minister, expressed a fussy dismay over the interna-

tional implications of the situation. The Canadians, including
the secretary of the British High Commissioner, were round-
ed up by the RCMP and the British intelligence agency, MI-5,
attended to Veall and May. May was sent to prison as the chief
perpetrator of the crime. It was unknown at the time, but MI-5
had been thoroughly penetrated by Russian spies.

Apparently, it had been May who, with Veall's help, had
removed the eleven milligrams of plutonium. It was said at the
time that his reward from the Russians was a bottle of scotch.
The theft had been done not for money but as a matter of principle. May's sympathies had been communist in England and,
despite his commitments to the British government and to the
project, his first concern was to help the Russians. After the
war, it became clear that, even with the rigid security practised
in the Manhattan Project, sympathizers managed to get a great
deal of information to the Russians. The security breach came
not from one of the anticipated sources but from human sim-
plicity and idealism.

————

The involvement of Canadians should not have been the surprise that it was. The long years of the Depression in Canada
leading up to the war had bred a generation ready to try any
political system that might hold out relief from the hardship
prevalent throughout the country. The leader of the Communist Party of Canada, Tim Buck, was an excellent speaker who
held many of the younger generation in his sway. Canada had
sent a battalion of volunteers to fight on the side of the communist Republicans in the Spanish civil war, and many of the
young men who volunteered for service in World War II were
sympathetic, if not committed, to communist political philos-
ophy. If there were no communist sympathizers among the
Canadian scientists in the Montreal Laboratory, it was perhaps
because young scientists in those days were generally apoli-
tical. Like the engineers of their generation, their schooling

and training was so rigorous as to leave little time for political meetings or outside activities of any kind while they were in university.

This is not to say that we did not sympathize with the Russians. For the greater part of the war they were our allies, and it was clear to everyone that they were bearing the brunt of the conflict. When the tide of war turned in Russia and the Germans, who had seemed until then invincible, were driven back on their own cities and towns, the Russians were hailed as heroes. We were ready to turn a blind eye on the deplorable excesses of the Stalin regime. It was only when the West came into intimate contact with the Russians that the many repulsive aspects of the Stalin regime became irrefutably obvious and caused despair and disillusionment among young Westerners who had been attracted to communism. Russia had been presented to young idealists in Canada as a paragon of social and economic justice by Tim Buck and others like him. The reality proved to be quite otherwise.

Very little of this was brought out during the war, though isolated instances might have forewarned the West. The Russians were accustomed, for instance, to low standards of safety and control; though they could be a charming people, they had little consideration for human rights or even for human life. A Russian delegation of arms experts visiting the munitions plant at Valcartier terrified the managers of the plant by disdaining what were considered basic safety precautions. It was an inviolate principle that steel objects were to be excluded from the plant for fear that a spark might be struck that would initiate an explosion. To the horror of the managers, the Russians drew knives from their briefcases and began testing the quality of cordite sheets by shaving strips off them.

It is idle to speculate as to what might have transpired had the Russians been made partners in the development of atomic energy instead of excluded by enforced secrecy, but the possibilities are interesting. Surely, they would have displayed less distrust and suspicion. Partnership with the West would have done much to encourage higher standards of design and safety in all aspects of atomic energy development. The dreadful accident at Chernobyl might never have happened. That it did happen brought home to the Russians that they were paying a terrible price for their isolation. The first-hand evidence of Western superiority in the technical and medical aspects of the problems at Chernobyl did much to convince the Russians that their vaunted science and industry had in fact languished under the communist regime and began the process of transformation that has led to the more open Russian society of today. If there had been partnership instead of secrecy and isolation, transformation might have begun fifty years sooner.

——————

Speculation aside, it is to the credit of both countries that Canada and Russia entered in January 1964 into a joint agreement for the exchange of information on the peaceful uses of atomic energy. This arose from the contacts made at the Atoms for Peace international conferences held in Geneva in 1955 and 1958. Whether the information received by the Rus-sians was of any use to them is a matter open to question, as Russia never entered to any great extent the field of heavy water/natural uranium reactors. Chalk River gained considerably by introduction to the Russian alloy development program. The Russians had developed, independent of the West, an alloy of zirconium with 2.5 per cent niobium, which could be used in heavy water reactors operating at temperatures of 300 degrees Celsius and above. This proved to be ideal for the CANDU power reactors then being designed, and Canada initiated a program of development that led to the extensive use of Zr-2.5%Nb alloys in CANDU reactors.

Social and technical contacts with the Russians arising from the 1964 agreement gave us Canadians the first inklings of the gap between the public perception of the Russians and the Russians as they actually were. We found that we had more in common with them than we had supposed. Their young scientists were just as impatient and scornful of bureaucratic interference as we were, and their opinions of their political leaders were simply unprintable. Ray Burge, head of public relations, and I hosted a group of them for AECL one evening at the Royal York Hotel in Toronto in 1966. I was to take them to AECL's Douglas Point project on Lake Huron the following day. I had rented a suite and laid on refreshments, sandwiches, and a bar. I had also brought along my harmonica, on which I played a few pre-war Russian songs, much to their delight. They balked at the Smirnoff vodka, however: "Na, na! Imperialist vodka!" A couple of them raced up to their rooms and returned with long, thin bottles containing what they called "real vodka." The party became merry, and the next thing I recall was waking up, fully dressed, on the couch. A glance at my watch told me it was 8:15 in the morning. The limousine to take us to Lake Huron was scheduled to leave the Royal York at 8:30. I dashed down to the lobby to find the Russians looking bright and rested and ready to go. I got them into the limousine and found I had to sit at the very back. Burge was nowhere to be seen. The drive from downtown Toronto to Kincardine, just east of Lake Huron, takes three hours. Weaving up and down and around in the back of the limousine for the first two hours was the hardest thing I have ever done. By the third hour I was beginning to feel I might survive. If the Russians noticed anything, they were too polite to mention it.

They were evidently captives of a rigid hierarchical system that inhibited their ability to give us information on technical subjects. Unless the scientist who had written the report was present, the results of that report could not be transmitted, or so they said. Others would not furnish information, except in the most general terms, on the work of an absent colleague.

Canadians had no such inhibitions, and the members of Russian delegations usually departed from Chalk River laden with twenty or more reports apiece. An offer to send the reports of this group by mail was rejected with cries of "Na! Na! We nyever get in mail! Send by deeplomatic bag!"

And so it was on one dark November afternoon in Ottawa that I, as the officer responsible for the party, knocked at the door of the Russian embassy with a great bundle of scientific reports to be transmitted by "deeplomatic" bag. Canadian suspicion of the Russians was such at that time that two large brick houses on Charlotte Street across from the embassy had blinds perpetually drawn to hide the RCMP officers and their surveillance operations. As the door of the embassy opened and I was admitted with my bundle of documents, I could feel those surveillance cameras boring into my back.

4

Nuclear Reactors

"They've a thing they call the "pile" at the Plant.
Well, I'd like to say I've seen it but I can't.
They say that when she really goes all the boys take off
*   their clothes*
And enjoy Atomic Energy!"

                                    The Deep River Song

The water of the Ottawa River, perhaps through contact with the bark of innumerable trees, is the colour of weak tea. The water in the river itself gives the appearance of being crystal clear, but in a glass held up to the light it is unmistakably faintly brown. This was distressful to the more squeamish residents of Deep River, but was taken in stride by the older inhabitants of the Valley. "It mixes wonderfully with rye," Murray Williams, a well-known Pembroke lawyer, used to say. Nevertheless, an impending visit of the Queen in 1953 caused the city of Ottawa, which draws its water from the river, to install a new water treatment plant. The thought of a tubful of brownish water for the Queen gave the city officials qualms. There had even been reports of small fish delivered through water taps in the city.

Ottawa River water was to be used to cool the NRX reactor, the centrepiece of the Chalk River project. The pumphouse and the water treatment plant were among the first buildings to be completed on the site. NRX was a step into the unknown, and it was uncertain whether river water would have to be treated before being used to cool the reactor. As it turned out, NRX proved to be just as adaptable to the river water as the older inhabitants of the Valley, and the water treatment plant was not used except as a filter for the cooling water.

————.

In principle, NRX was to be similar to ZEEP. But whereas ZEEP produced the energy of a single flashlight bulb, NRX was to produce ten megawatts, the energy of ten thousand electric hot plates, all turned up to maximum heat. The reactor was to operate at temperatures only slightly above room temperature, so all this heat had to be carried away by the cooling water.

As with ZEEP, rods of pure uranium metal were to be suspended in a regular array vertically in a large tank of pure heavy water. The spacing between the rods was carefully calculated to make maximum use of the neutrons produced from fission. Each rod had to be cooled individually and sheathed, both to protect the uranium from contact with the cooling water and to contain the highly radioactive fission products in the uranium. The cooling water had to be kept to the minimum, since too much ordinary water in the reactor could not be tolerated. The cooling water also could not be allowed to come into contact with the precious heavy water, since this would degrade the latter and render it useless for maintaining the fission reaction. Neither leakage nor evaporation of heavy water could be tolerated. Millions of dollars were involved. Only those materials of construction that would not capture too many of the precious neutrons could be used for the construction of the reactor. NRX, though simple in principle, became an exquisite problem in engineering and design. The details given above are a mere outline of the difficulties that had to be overcome.

————.

Much of the original engineering and design work was done while the project was still situated in the University of Montreal, and engineers on the U.K. staff, particularly C.W. Gilbert and Harold Tongue, contributed mightily to the success of the design. Engineering drawings were made under the direc-

tion of the chief architect of the university, who was happy to
work as a draftsman. He had fallen out with the Duplessis government over the design of the university (it was very sensibly
all under one roof). There had been, to be sure, some architec-
tural gaffes. The university's central tower was capped with a
cupola designed to take an astronomical telescope but which,
together with the tower, gave the unmistakable impression of a
phallic monument. The cupola was entirely useless for an
observatory, since the tower was so susceptible to vibration that
a telescope could not be used in it.

Engineers from Fraser Brace were drawn in to the NRX project later, as were engineers from NRC and DIL. It was a learning
process for everyone, and it says much for the quality of the
engineers involved and their cooperation with the scientists
that NRX became an outstanding success. Success was not
immediate and the reactor did not become operational until
1947, but considering the fact that this was Canada's first experience in building a large atomic reactor, the progress made
was impressive.

·———·

The gradual withdrawal of the U.K. staff from Chalk River
and Montreal began in 1945 and was practically complete by
1948, when research facilities at Harwell, near Oxford, became
available. Sir John Cockcroft had been appointed head of the
U.K. establishment and departed early to supervise the new
organization, leaving the direction of the Canadian project
open. A search was made for a Canadian scientist to fill the
position, but without success. Most of the Canadians employed
in the project at the time were in their twenties and thirties and
had yet to make their mark. An attempt was made to attract
Walter Zinn, a Canadian who was director of the Argonne
Laboratory of the U.S. Atomic Energy Commission. He, however, had put down roots in the Chicago area, was flourishing
at his job, and could not be persuaded to begin all over again

at Chalk River. The search then turned to Britain, where Dr
W.B. Lewis had become free of his responsibilities as director
of Telecommunications Research Establishment, a wartime
venture that was shutting down. Lewis had been a colleague of
Cockcroft at Cambridge and had been part of that group at the
Cavendish Laboratory that had revolutionized atomic science
in the years before the war. He was chosen to head the Chalk
River Project.

One Canadian who, rather surprisingly, had been passed
over in this process was George C. Laurence, a physicist with
the National Research Council who had been with the Project since its earliest days. He was a fine-looking man with a
well-shaped, aristocratic head on broad shoulders and an "out-
doors" look about him. He was married and had two daugh-
ters. As a student, Laurence had been an "exhibitioner" at
Cavendish and had done brilliant work on the absorption of
X-rays in matter. His papers in the *Canadian Journal of Physics*
were held up as examples of originality and elegant clarity. In
the months leading up to the war he had started on his own initiative a series of experiments in the NRC laboratory in Ottawa
to test the feasibility of producing a self-sustaining nuclear
reaction in a mixture of uranium oxide and graphite. That he
was unsuccessful was due to the impurity of his materials and
the small scale of his experiments, which were conducted
secretly, on his own time and with limited resources. He, more
than any Canadian other than Zinn, within or outside of the
Project, appeared qualified for the directorship. It is perhaps a
measure of the man that he did not resign from the Project on
being passed over. It must have been a bitter pill to swallow
and small compensation to remain as director of a physics division. He was later appointed president of the Atomic Energy
Control Board.

Wilfrid Bennett Lewis was an entirely different human being.
Still a bachelor at thirty-eight years, he had the reputation of

being married to his work. His grasp was encyclopedic and his output prodigious. He almost single-handedly brought the Chalk River Project to world prominence in the field of atomic energy. The scientists working under him were often at odds with his methods of leadership, however. L.G. Cook, head of the Chemistry Branch, compared his management technique to that of a baseball coach who pushes each player aside in turn and plays the position as he thinks it should be played. Whatever may be said about Lewis's management methods, they had the effect of keeping the scientific staff on their toes. Anyone coming to report to him on developments in his own field, be it physics, chemistry, metallurgy, engineering, or any other branch of science, had better be on solid ground with his subject if he was to avoid humiliation at the hands of the director. Not that the humiliation was inflicted with any intention to hurt. Lewis seemed to be immune to considerations of human pride or vanity. He merely stated what to him seemed obvious. Ernie Renton, the plant doctor, regularly treated with tranquilizers certain individuals after their interviews with the director. If Lewis had a guiding principle, it was that any problem could be solved by physics, if only the physicist was prepared to put his mind to it.

I remember once remarking to Archie Robertson, a colleague in Chemistry and Metallurgy, when I was working on nuclear fuel development at Chalk River, "It seems amazing that so few people in this field can see the problem as it really is." Archie thought for a moment and replied, "It's easy enough to see the problem when you have someone who can tell you where to look." He meant W.B. Lewis.

Lewis never left an account of his impressions on coming to the Chalk River Project. Coming as he did from an organization that was on the cutting edge of developments in electronics, he was clearly horrified by the quality of electronic equipment with which the Project was furnished and, as one of his first actions, imported a former colleague, Norman Moodie, to set things right. Electronics had been the domain of Herbert F. Freundlich, a youthful member of the U.K. staff known as "Uncle Herbert" to his minions. His approach to the development of electronic instruments was that of a Cambridge professor, comfortable with old-fashioned components. The scalers, devices for counting the electrical pulses produced by radioactive radiation, used the ancient "electronic eye" tube to count the pulses. As a scale of ten required nine of these tubes (the tenth pulse triggered a mechanical register) and each tube was four inches long, the housing for the device was large and bulky. The high voltage supplies were also potentially dangerous, as one young Canadian physicist, D.H.W. Kirkwood, could testify. The 450-volt D.C. shock he received sent the fifty-pound voltage supply twenty feet across the laboratory as a reaction of the muscles of his arms before he passed out – to be revived some minutes later, none the worse, one hopes, for his experience. Kirkwood shortly thereafter left physics for a career in the Department of External Affairs in Ottawa, seeking – presumably – a less hazardous occupation.

There was no space within the fenced enclosure for an electronics laboratory, but Moodie set up shop in an old Fraser Brace dormitory and was soon working wonders. The scaling circuits, which had stood like isolated towers on the laboratory benches, became small and compact and fitted into standard electronic racks so that clusters of them could be used for more complicated experiments. No one ever received another shock from a voltage supply. What is more, the equipment looked professional.

———————

W.B. Lewis arrived in Chalk River in 1946. Known as "Ben" to his family and English friends, he became "W.B." among the staff at Chalk River. He dwelt in one of the executive houses in Deep River on Beach Avenue on the shore of the Ottawa, a stretch known as "Skunk Hollow" to the lesser mortals of the Project. He shared the street with other notables such as G.C.

W.B. Lewis at the unveiling on 18 June 1966 of the plaque
commemorating the start-up of ZEEP in September of 1945.
This photograph was chosen because it is an excellent
portrait of Lewis in his working clothes. He had nothing to
do with ZEEP, which was brought to completion under the
direction of Lew Kowarski, one of the Free French scientists at Chalk River, a fact that is missing from the plaque.
In 1966 Lewis was vice president, Research at Chalk River
and had already made the centre one of international importance in the scientific world. His expression radiates success. AECL Photo No. 6606-5356-1

Laurence and J.L. Gray, a future president of the organization. Lewis was soon joined by his mother, Isoline Lewis, who lived out the rest of her life in Deep River. It was ever her fond hope that her son would marry, and a special effort was made to interest him in each of his secretaries. Things looked hopeful in the case of Agnes Comiskey, until she met young Ron Taplin, one of Moodie's English imports. (She eventually became Mrs Blair McGuffie.) Others who knew Lewis well were as sure as one can ever be that he would never marry.

W.B. Lewis and his mother were strong supporters of the Anglican church in Deep River, and it might have assuaged the feelings of those who had to rely upon Ernie Renton's tranquilizers to see the director upon his knees, as he often was, reciting the general Confession of the Morning Prayer: "...But thou, O Lord, have mercy upon us, miserable offenders. Spare though them, O God, which confess their faults. Restore thou them that are penitent..."

———

Lewis's first concern was, of course, to get NRX up and running. No one - physicist, engineer, operator, or electrician - had ever had anything to do with an installation as sophisticated as NRX. Techniques and procedures had to be developed, complex measurements made, expensive materials to be managed (at one point gallons of precious heavy water went down the drain as the result of a supervisor's mistake), and, above all, staff had to be trained. The quality of staff was generally excellent; tradesmen, operators and riggers, superintendents, all, with few exceptions, were extremely capable men. Some had been loggers a few years before.

Added to these complexities was the question of protection from penetrating radiations. NRX itself was so suitably shielded that it could be approached at close range even when operating at full power, but any material exposed within the reactor - the fuel elements themselves, for instance - became dangerously radioactive and had to be handled by special techniques. Levels of radiation in Building 100, where NRX was housed, were monitored continuously and regular checks were made by the Health Radiation Branch to detect contamination from spills or other untoward incidents.

The safety of staff was a primary concern. Operators and tradesmen were made to disrobe to their underclothes in a locker room and change into white coveralls before reporting for work. Shoes and socks were also removed and plant issue of so-called "active" footwear put on. The issued shoes were of black leather, with steel safety toes, and the tips were painted bright orange to identify them as "active" and possibly to discourage pilfering. All this active clothing was monitored for radioactivity before being sent to a specialized laundry. Workers were similarly monitored before being released from shift. If the slightest radioactive contamination was found, they were required to shower until it was removed.

When workers were to enter a region of known radioactive contamination, bright-coloured rubbers were donned over the "active" shoes as added protection and removed, monitored, and cleaned upon leaving the contaminated area. In some cases, rubbers were exchanged for a second set of rubbers in areas suspected of severe contamination; these were "double-rubber areas." The company safe in Building 400, the administration building, was referred to by some wag as a "double-rubber area" after an amorous couple was caught there, in *flagrante delicto*, after a particularly long coffee break.

The so-called "active change rooms" were put to good use when, in 1952, a serious accident occurred to NRX that left the reactor building contaminated with radioactivity from ruptured and melted fuel rods. Cleaning up the mess meant calling on all men in the plant as well as units of the Canadian armed forces and the U.S. Navy to put in time scrubbing to remove radioactive contamination in preparation for rehabil-

itation of the reactor. Many of us saw for the first time our colleagues in a state of complete undress, a sight that in some cases
was particularly illuminating.

————.

To add to the technical difficulties to be overcome, Lewis was
faced with rebellion by the younger members of his professional staff. Many had stayed on after the war because of the
promise of opportunities to do research in a new field. Science
in Canada had never been like this. Even in large universities
like Toronto and McGill, equipment was often hard to come
by, projects were done on a shoestring, and funding was almost
non-existent. The Chalk River Project was quite otherwise.
Funding was seldom a problem. In most fields it was a case of
"ask and it shall be given you." Most of the Canadians had
never been involved in "Big Science" before and those fresh
out of universities were like children in a candy shop. The
opportunities for research were myriad and each anticipated
a brilliant career in his own field.

This was all very well and was to some extent encouraged in
the period after the war while NRX was still under construction
and commissioning, but it was obvious to Lewis and to others
in senior positions that the Project needed a focus if it was to
survive and that the obvious focus was the development of
atomic energy. This meant that the physics done at Chalk River
should be the physics of atomic energy, chemistry the chemistry of atomic energy, metallurgy the metallurgy of atomic energy, and so forth. This smacked too much of industrial
science for many, particularly those young and recently out of
university. Led by a young physicist, Donald Brunton, in the
summer of 1948 they called for public discussion of the future
of the Project. Meetings were held in the main lecture hall in
which Lewis was pitted against these dissidents. He proved to
be more than a match for them. He argued persuasively that
there was as much science and as much research to be done on

reactors like NRX as there was in any field, that scientific careers and reputations were as promising there as in any other field, probably more so at this time in the history of atomic energy, and that, in any case, their talents and abilities were needed to make the Project a success.

He was, as usual, right. It is a measure of his success that Chalk River became an international centre of excellence, not only in atomic energy but in many associated fields, including mathematics, physics, chemistry, metallurgy, ceramics, and engineering. It became the practice to invite university professors for two- or three-month sabbaticals during the summer and it was rarely found that these teachers were as advanced in their field as their opposite numbers in the Project. And indeed, as the Chalk River laboratories matured, individual projects not directly related to the reactor were supported and encouraged when it was demonstrated that they had promise. John Davies, a brilliant young chemist, developed a new school of investigation into the structure of matter. Alistair Cameron became a cosmologist of world reknown and later a director of the Harvard Observatory. Bert Brockhouse recently won a Nobel Prize in physics for work he had begun at Chalk River. Many went on to major university positions in Canada and the United States.

The conversion of Don Brunton must also have been complete, for within a period of six months he left the Project and, with an associate, N.Z. Alcock (of later peace research fame), founded Isotope Enterprises in Oakville, Ontario, to develop the industrial and medical applications of radioactive isotopes produced in NRX.

————

Radioactive isotopes have become such an important development parallel to the development of atomic energy that they deserve a history to themselves. An isotope of any element has the same chemical properties as the element. Thus deuterium,

The Chalk River Nuclear Laboratories on a winter's night in 1966. The twin stacks are for exhausting the ventilation air from the buildings. The black-tipped stack is for the plutonium extraction plant, which was discontinued in 1947 when it was established that Canada would concentrate on the peaceful uses of atomic energy. Lew Kowarski's ZEEP was put together in the small, barn-like building in the foreground. The first large building houses the NRX reactor. The building between it and the Ottawa River houses the NRU reactor. The camera is looking downriver. Oiseau Rock is on the Quebec shore just to the left of the black-tipped stack. The point stretching out on the Ontario side is the Pointe au Baptême, so called because the Aboriginal families used to bring their children there to be baptized by visiting French priests. The story has it that on one fearful occasion an eagle snatched up an unattended baby and flew with it across the river to the top of the cliff at Oiseau Rock, which got its name from the incident. AECL Photo No. 6104-2594 the heavy isotope of hydrogen, has chemical properties identical with hydrogen (this is a simplification, but will serve the purpose) but has twice the mass. "Heavy water" is water in which deuterium takes the place of hydrogen. It is rare because deuterium forms such a tiny fraction of the hydrogen found in nature.

During the period of wartime and post-war secrecy the code word for heavy water was "polymer," which may have been the source of the rumour that Chalk River was to be a polymer plant. If so, it was an example of the success of code words in maintaining secrecy.

All naturally occurring elements are usually mixtures of isotopes, identical chemically but having different masses. Uranium, code word X-metal, is no exception. As found in nature, uranium is a mixture of three isotopes, of masses 234, 235, and 238. The proportion of U-234 is so small as to be negligible. Even the proportion of U-235 is less than one per cent; it is U-235 that is of interest to our story, for it is the isotope that undergoes fission when exposed to neutrons. U-238 can capture neutrons but does not fission, though neutron capture leads to the production of plutonium, some isotopes of which do fission. Natural uranium is almost pure U-238. The Manhattan Project in the United States was devoted in large part to the separation of U-235, to provide a stockpile of fissile uranium. This was a vast and enormously costly process quite beyond the means of the Chalk River Project. As was shown by Kowarski in 1939, it is possible to produce a self-sustaining fission reaction by surrounding natural uranium with heavy water, which greatly enhances the probability of fission. This was the course taken by Chalk River in designing Canadian reactors.

————

Without going into a detailed description of atomic structure, it should be stated at this point that the processes of fission and the emission of neutrons and alpha particles, beta particles, and gamma rays are processes occuring in the core, or nucleus, of the atom. It is in the nucleus that the mass of the atom is concentrated and it is from transformations in the nucleus that the energy of fission is derived. The term "atomic energy" is more precisely "nuclear energy," though in the following chapters I shall use both terms interchangeably.

Neutrons not used in producing fission of U-235 can be used to produce radioactive isotopes. Many elements exposed to neutrons capture neutrons and produce new isotopes, and many of these new isotopes are radioactive. That is, they emit alpha, beta, or gamma radiation, or combinations of them. There are several ways in which this property is important. Two of these are discussed below.

Instruments for the detection of penetrating radiation are extremely sensitive and capable of detecting individual emissions from radioactive substances. The sensitivity is thus far greater than can be obtained by any other method. If one wishes to detect mercury contamination of water, for example, one needs only to subject the water sample to neutron irradiation and look for radiations characteristic of radioactive mercury isotopes. A mere trace of mercury diluted in millions of gallons of water can be detected in this way. The technique is called "activation analysis" and has been highly developed in many laboratories, as in those at the universities of Toronto and Dalhousie. It is a great boon to environmental science.

Similarly, if one wishes to follow the uptake of nitrogen or potassium in a plant or tree, one can expose the roots to a solution in which radioactive nitrogen or radioactive potassium has been added to the fertilizer and follow with instruments the progress of the radioactive material through the plant or tree. The radioactive material traces the movement of normal nitrogen or potassium since it is chemically indistinguishable from them. Studies of this kind, using radioactive tracers, have been used to determine at which stage of plant growth specific fertilizers are most important. If the leaf of a plant so treated is pressed against a photographic plate in a darkroom, it produces an image on the plate of the distribution of the radioactive material in the leaf.

A second type of application makes use of the effectiveness of penetrating radiation in destroying cancerous tissue. For example, the thyroid gland tends to take up iodine. Certain diseases of the thyroid can be treated effectively by dosing the patient with radioactive iodine, which when taken up by the thyroid produces a concentration of the radioactive iodine in the diseased organ and subjects the diseased tissue to the effects of penetrating radiation from the iodine. Since cancerous tissue is much less resistant than healthy tissue to destruction by the radiation, it is selectively destroyed. The radioactive iodine eventually disappears by a process called "radioactive decay."

Such applications merely indicate the beginning of the possibilities opened in biology, medicine, and environmental science by the use of radioactive isotopes. These possibilities had been recognized from the time the design of NRX was begun and radioactive isotope production was included as one of the elements of design. The commercial production of isotopes began early in the history of the Project. A special branch devoted to isotope production gradually evolved into a separate and now private company, Commercial Products, known today as MDS-Nordion, with a market in which it supplies some 50,000 customers worldwide in hospitals, research institutions, and industry with radioactive isotopes for a myriad of applications. The production of radioactive isotopes is thus a major benefit accompanying the use of atomic power.

5

Nuclear Applications

"Oh, the day, the day, the happy, happy day
When I buy my "One Horse Atom Shay"!
I'll "pull the rods" and let her go off to Pembroke
* through the snow,*
Runnin' on Atomic Energy!"

The Deep River Song

It would be intriguing if the wood-burning *Oiseau*, now just a memory, were one day replaced by a vessel running on atomic power, offering – as did the *Oiseau* – tours up and down the majestic Ottawa River between Pembroke and Les Rapides des Joachims. The possibility seems remote, yet propulsion by a small reactor would not be out of the question. But what a difference between the two! The SS *Pontiac*, the wood-burning ferry between Pembroke and Allumette Island, which operated until 1956, puffing out from the slip in Pembroke in a shower of sparks from the tall funnel, recalled what travel on the *Oiseau* must have been like. By contrast, an atomic-powered vessel would slide silently through the water, coming close to the Quebec shore without frightening wildlife. There would be no shower of sparks issuing from a funnel. There would be no funnel. There would be no stops at jetties along the way to take on fuel. One charge of fuel would last the season, or several seasons if desired. Stops would be for sight-seeing: Fort William, the old Hudson Bay post; the three-hundred-foot sheer cliff at Oiseau Rock for a picnic stop and an excursion to the little lake at the top of the rock; the community of Deep River, now spread well beyond the confines of the DIL village;

Colonel Fraser's historic property at Fraser's Landing; the rapids at des Joachims, now confined by the great hydroelectric project at Rolphton. How fitting it would be: the power of wood replaced by the power of the atom, employed on the river intimately related to both.

————·

Putting aside, for the moment, the many practical, political, and psychological problems such an imagined future raises, it should be said at once that it became clear from the earliest considerations of propulsion using atomic power that watercraft were the prime candidates. Not that all sorts of imaginative uses were not considered, ranging from railway engines and passenger aircraft all the way to the *Orion* Project, which envisaged interplanetary travel in a spaceship driven by successive atomic explosions. Although ideas like *Orion* actually attracted study, they were eventually abandoned, but the feasibility of ship propulsion was never in question.

The Chalk River Project became an early participant in the development of ship propulsion, thanks to the NRX reactor. NRX had been started, after months of painstaking preparation, at 06:13 hours on 22 July 1947. It was a beautiful summer morning and a great day for Canada. Lewis and his immediate staff, physicists D.G. Hurst and A.G. Ward, had taken up positions in a superintendent's office, away from the control room where four scientists and a group of operators were gradually increasing the depth of the heavy water and measuring the corresponding reactivity of the reactor. Readings were relayed to Lewis and his staff, who plotted them on a blackboard in the office. A self-sustaining reaction was achieved as the sun rose over the cliffs on the Quebec shore. As an indication of the care and precision that had gone into the design of NRX, calculations had indicated that "divergence," that is, a self-sustaining reaction, would be achieved at a depth of heavy water of 168 centimetres. Divergence actually began at 168.5 centimetres.

What a triumph of design in a new and unknown field! The story was told in the data plotted on the blackboard. Someone, probably Lewis, had the forethought to scrawl "DO NOT ERASE" at the top of the board. A photograph of the board with this historic data remains in the Project archives.

NRX went on to prove itself a remarkably useful instrument. Not only had it been designed for maximum flexibility for the production of radioactive isotopes for medical and industrial use, but it was easily adapted for a number of important scientific experiments and industrial development projects. Its main advantage stemmed from the fact that, being a heavy water reactor, it had an intense neutron flux distributed evenly over a large volume, making it ideal for a wide range of experiments. NRX became a magnet, drawing atomic energy experiments of all kinds from every country doing work in the field.

Just as its usefulness was becoming widely known, an accident occurred on 12 December 1952 that threatened to terminate the life of the reactor and possibly that of the Chalk River Project. The cooling water to one of the fuel elements had been replaced by air to facilitate certain measurements at zero reactor power. On restoring the reactor to normal power, an error was made in calculating the level of heavy water needed. More heavy water was introduced than was needed, and this caused the reactor power to rise. This should have been stopped immediately by lowering shut-off rods, rods of neutron-absorbing material, into the reactor. But the rods did not function as planned and the reactor power rose rapidly to well above the designed power of NRX. Someone in the control room quickly pressed the button that dumped the heavy water out of the reactor into its holding tank. This promptly shut down the reactor, but by then the uranium in the air-cooled element had already melted at white heat, destroying the cooling channel in which it was situated. Several other fuel rods were being cooled with temporary fittings for the experiment and the power surge

damaged these as well. The gaseous radioactivity released
was carried by the ventilating air out the stack and high over
the Project, where it tripped all the radiation alarms in the
plant, signaling a general emergency. For the only time in its
history, the siren of the steam plant by the river sounded an
evacuation of the plant. People responded with varying degrees
of calm. A bulldozer operator leapt off his machine, leaving it
running, climbed over the nearest fence mindless of barbed
wire, and was never seen again. Buses and cars were boarded in
fairly good order, but once on the road out of the plant it was
every man for himself. A solid stream of traffic, two abreast,
hastened along the road toward Chalk River, pushing to one
side anyone coming the other way.

In one of the buses B.G. Harvey – he who had done so much
to establish the micro-chemistry of plutonium – said to me that
this was it, the end of NRX and the Chalk River Project. Acting
upon this conviction he soon left Chalk River and moved his
family to the United States, where he became a distinguished
member of the team of Glenn T. Seaborg, at the University of
California at Berkeley.

————

The accident signaled an unpropitious start for a new organization, Atomic Energy of Canada Limited, which had been
established the previous April to take over the Project from
the National Research Council. The industrial aspects of the
Project had been increasing, and though administration under
NRC had been a successful wartime measure, the work now to
be undertaken was best done by a crown corporation, organized along company lines. By now the misgivings of the scientists who had opposed "commercialization" had been
completely tamed. Dr C.J. Mackenzie, who had been president
of NRC during the war and whose no-nonsense approach had
done much to win over those Americans who distrusted the
Europeans, was appointed president of AECL. W.B. Lewis was
made vice president in charge of research.

Mackenzie was of course besieged by the media when news of the accident began to raise a panic among the adjacent townships. He was in Ottawa when the accident occurred, so had no details, but put on a brave front by telling reporters that the incident was a "pinhole leak" in the reactor. By then the basement of NRX was waist-deep in water. Fortunately, no one thought of saying "Some pin! Some hole!"

B.G. Harvey was wrong about both NRX and the Project. By using ingenuity and determination, calling on the help of everyone in the plant (though the work was done mainly by AECL Operations), the Canadian Army, the RCAF, and the U.S. Navy (including a young Lt Jimmy Carter), and rigorously controlling exposure to radiation at every stage of the operation, all radioactive spills were cleaned up, the damaged components of the reactor were replaced, damaged fuel elements were removed, a new reactor vessel was put in place, improvements to controls and shielding were made, and the reactor was recharged and restarted, all in a matter of fourteen months. What had seemed inconceivably difficult proved to be possible. Hurst and Ward, reporting on the accident to the 1955 Geneva Conference on the Peaceful Uses of Atomic Energy, said that problems considered insuperable before the accident were now seen as merely difficult and annoying.

A rapid heavy water dump became a feature much promoted by W.B. Lewis for future power reactors. However, design calculations showed it to be too slow to be effective in the large reactors to be built in the future and other, more dependable fast shut-downs were devised.

————.

If NRX had been useful before, it was now even more so, for the accident had shown that the design had been so conservative that the reactor could easily be operated at forty megawatts instead of the designed ten megawatts. (Conservatism had been intentional in the original design and power had been increased to thirty Mw even before the accident.) This resulted in a correspondingly higher density of neutrons. The reactor once again attracted experiments from several quarters. Of these the most important, both from the standpoint of outcomes and from the learning experience it gave AECL staff, was the development of fuel for the U.S. nuclear submarine program.

————

The U.S. Navy had contracts with both General Electric and Westinghouse for the development of submarines propelled by reactors using atomic power. The General Electric contract was for a vessel, *Seawolf*, powered by a "boiling water reactor," that is, one in which the water was allowed to boil in the reactor and the steam used directly to operate a turbine that propelled the craft. Though the concept had certain advantages – and eventually proved to be superior in terms of stealth of the submarine – development was difficult and the time scale so drawn out that unkind critics labeled the submarine *Dockwolf*.

The Westinghouse contract was to build a submarine powered by a pressurized water reactor of Westinghouse design. The water in the reactor was pressurized to prevent boiling and the heat generated in it by the nuclear reaction was made to generate steam in a second circuit connected to the turbine. The submarine propelled by this system was to be called *Nautilus* after the ship in the Jules Verne science fiction novel *Twenty Thousand Leagues under the Sea*. It was the Westinghouse team that came to Chalk River to make use of NRX.

Both contracts were administered by one of the most colourful and outrageous individuals in the history of the U.S. Navy, Admiral Hyman G. Rickover. Rickover made a point of dominating every conversation by the sheer weight of his intellect, irrespective of rank or position. He was avoided by those who could avoid him and feared by those who could not. His very maintenance of his active role in the U.S. Navy is a matter for wonder, for he was reappointed by successive presidents until, at the age of eighty-one, he was finally retired by

Ronald Reagan. Even at that age he rose at 6 a.m. and put in a full day's work.

David Lewis, chairman of General Dynamics Corporation, whose Electric Boat Division at Groton, Connecticut, was under contract to produce *Nautilus*, was required to report to Rickover every morning by telephone on the state of progress of the contract, and he did. The mere mention of Rickover's name to members of the General Electric team produced visible palpitations among the more sensitive, one of whom claimed that if he had not been on his toes, Rickover would have walked right over him.

The Westinghouse team had apparently worked out a *modus vivendi* with the admiral that involved doing everything on a grand scale. Based at its Bettis Plant in Pittsburgh, Westinghouse maintained a team at Chalk River under the direction of Kenneth Vogel, a competent young engineer. The team's task was to supervise the testing of nuclear fuel for the *Nautilus* in the NRX reactor. The team was in daily contact with Pittsburgh by telephone for hours at a time and it was rumoured that the monthly phone bill was in the thousands of dollars. Zirconium, largely a laboratory curiosity until the *Nautilus* program, was to be used as the sheathing material for the fuel. It was the only metal with a low absorption for neutrons (leaving more for the fission process) that could be used at the water temperatures intended. The then current means of production was by a laboratory process patented by professors van Arkel and de Boer. The product was very pure "crystal bar zirconium," but was produced in amounts no more than a pound or so at a time. Visitors to the plant in Pittsburgh with suitable security clearance were shown a $50-million installation in which the van Arkel units were repeated hundreds of times over to produce a respectable amount of zirconium.

Dr Ben Lustman, the director of metallurgical development at Westinghouse and an authority on zirconium, was largely

responsible for the development of Zircaloy-2, an alloy of zirconium containing 2.5 per cent tin and traces of iron, nickel,
and chromium. Zircaloy-2 made possible the fuel sheathing for
the high temperatures required in ship reactors, yet remained
sufficiently "transparent" to neutrons. True to their predilection for secrecy and security, the Americans code-named
Zircaloy "Myrna Loy," the name of a lovely and winsome movie
actress very popular at the time. Ms Loy was entertained, when
secrecy was no longer necessary, at a special banquet put on
for the occasion. It was said that she was very touched to have
contributed to alloy development in this way.

The prototype fuel elements for the *Nautilus* needed to be
tested at the temperatures proposed for the ship reactor, but
these temperatures were far above the temperature of NRX. An
ingenious technique was devised: the test fuel was contained
in a steel tube, or "test section," that was mounted in the central thimble of the reactor and supplied with its own closed circuit containing a circulating pump to circulate the water and
heaters to develop the required temperature. The test fuel
would receive the full neutron intensity of NRX but would be
maintained in water circulating at the temperature of the
Nautilus reactor.

This collaboration proved to be enormously important for
AECL. The circuit, or "loop," as it was called, was operated by
AECL staff, who also monitored the behaviour of the fuel in
close cooperation with Westinghouse. The groundwork was
laid for much of the development of Canada's own power reactor, CANDU. Chalk River became adept in testing fuel in loops,
both in NRX and later in the larger reactor, NRU. Loop chemistry and metallurgy became a Chalk River specialty, and
Chalk River loops were studied and copied wherever this type
of work was done. Loops were "loops" in Canada, Britain, and
the United States. Even in Italy a loop became "*il lupo*," to the

puzzlement of the uninitiated, since the word means "wolf" in Italian. Only the French, with the insularity characteristic of those times, preferred to use the French word "*la boucle*."

———————

Thanks to Westinghouse, AECL was at the vanguard of information on the water treatment necessary for reactors operating at high temperatures and incorporated this into the design of Canada's later power reactors. The *Nautilus* fuel in the NRX loop developed, over an irradiation of several months, a deposit on the fuel sheath that might interfere with the transfer of heat from the fuel to the coolant. The discovery of this deposit, which was given the acronym CRUD by Paul Cohen of Westinghouse (for Chalk River Unidentified Deposit), caused major concern to the *Nautilus* project, and telephone lines between Chalk River and Pittsburgh were burdened for weeks with frantic calls between the two centres. In due course it was demonstrated that CRUD was a deposit of iron oxide from the steel surfaces in the loop and could be avoided simply by making the coolant water slightly alkaline, as had been the established practice in steam plants for many years.

———————

The *Nautilus* was launched at the Groton shipyard of Electric Boat on 21 January 1954 at a ceremony attended by some 15,000 people. Mrs Eisenhower, wife of the president, was brought from Washington in a nine-car special train to perform the christening. It was a day plagued by fog and the 340-foot profile of the ship was barely visible to many of the crowd for a good part of the ceremony, but the sun came out and the fog dispersed as Mrs Eisenhower broke the champagne bottle over the bow and the sleek, tubular vessel slipped into the water. It was a moment to remember.

The *New York Times* correspondent, carried away by the occasion, lauded the ship's ability to cruise around the world without ever coming to the surface, a feat later immortalized by the American comedian Bob Newhart in his skit about the U.S. nuclear submarine U.S.S. *Codfish*:

CAPTAIN, just before surfacing at the end of a "two year underwater endurance" cruise: "I think we ought to give the cooks a standing ovation for the magnificent job they have done." (Silence) "You men want to stand now for the cooks ?" (Silence) "Come on now, let bygones be bygones..."

Fitted with the Westinghouse nuclear power plant and powered with the fuel developed in NRX, *Nautilus* eventually took to the high seas in a successful shake-down voyage. The propulsion system was revolutionary. It required no oxygen and could run for weeks, months if necessary, without the vessel's coming to the surface. The ship started to set records almost immediately. In eighty-four hours it traveled under water 1,300 miles, ten times farther than any submarine had traveled submerged. Other records followed: *Nautilus* maintained a speed under water of sixteen knots for over an hour, a record for any combat submarine. Admiral Rickover basked in the publicity given to this success and even deigned to visit Chalk River to pay his compliments to the part AECL had played in the venture. There was a reported clash of personalities between the admiral and W.B. Lewis, in which it must be admitted that Lewis came off second best. The admiral managed to catch him out on one or two obscure points of information and make him purple with rage by assuring him in public that the CANDU power reactor would be known as "the reactor of a thousand leaks." Then, having done what damage he could, the admiral departed.

W.B. Lewis had developed very friendly relations with the Electric Boat Company and its chairman, David Lewis, who had enormous respect for W.B.'s imagination and scientific competence. One wonders whether part of the attraction between them was a mutual abhorrence of the admiral.

Whatever Lewis's feelings may have been in the matter, the collaboration with Westinghouse gave an impetus to Chalk River's own plans for producing a reactor that could be used to generate power, most probably electrical power. The existence of Zircaloy-2 meant that the necessary material was at hand for constructing such a reactor and for sheathing the uranium fuel. (The development of the Russian zirconium-niobium alloy was to come later.) It now merely remained to design the system. That short sentence covers a staggering number of problems and considerations.

––––––––––

Meanwhile, the confidence gained with NRX had encouraged Lewis and the Project directors to embark in 1951 (that is, before the NRX accident) upon an even more ambitious reactor design. The Ottawa River water with which NRX was cooled stole some of the neutrons from the fission process. This could not be altered in NRX, but what if a reactor could be cooled with heavy water? This would be just as efficient a coolant as ordinary water, and would behave just like the heavy water surrounding the fuel in promoting fission without stealing neutrons from the process. One drawback would be the great cost of the heavy water; furthermore, it was one thing to contain the heavy water in a tank and quite another to pump it around in a circuit that furnished each fuel channel with flowing water for cooling. There would be a thousand joints that might leak, and though heavy water was now down to $90 a litre, no appreciable loss could be permitted. Even the initial investment in heavy water posed financial questions quite aside from the cost of building the reactor.

A prime feature of such a heavy water reactor is its efficient production of plutonium. It was probably W.B. Lewis who came up with the idea of financing the construction of the reactor with the sale of the plutonium. The obvious customer was the U.S. Atomic Energy Commission, which had embarked upon a massive nuclear weapons program. C.J. Mackenzie was encouraged to call upon his many influential contacts in Ottawa, including, of course, his minister, C.D. Howe.

Clarence Decatur Howe had become something of an institution during the war. As minister of Munitions and Supply, the war had made him an industrial czar whose influence pervaded every aspect of the war effort. It was he who, after the war, startled Canadians with the comment "What's a million?" Even on emerging victorious from the war, the country was still haunted by memories of the Depression and quite unprepared for extravagant expressions of this kind. Mackenzie made good use of his friendly acceptance by the Americans and succeeded in drawing up – with help from Lorne Gray, a future president of AECL – an agreement on the part of the USAEC to purchase the plutonium from the new reactor, though there was some hesitation about the price. Armed with this agreement and the estimates for the reactor, Howe obtained the backing of Cabinet to proceed with the project.

Variously regarded as a mad adventure in extravagance or as a technical *tour de force* without equal, NRU (for National Research Universal) was designed by G.C. Laurence's Physics Division and built by the C.D. Howe Company, a firm founded by the minister in the pre-war era. Official histories are careful to point out that "the Rt. Hon. C.D. Howe had severed his connections with the company many years before." If anyone had doubts about a conflict of interest he did not have the temerity to express them. It did not pay to cross C.D. Howe, just as it was a good thing to be one of Howe's "boys."

Chief engineer for C.D. Howe was Winnett Boyd, interestingly enough the scion of a family of lumber barons in Bobcaygeon, Ontario. He had won his reputation in the aircraft industry. Whereas NRX had been a wartime venture, done in secrecy and haste, scraping the barrel for materials and manpower, NRU showed what could be done by Canadian engineers and physicists, given the time and the money. Boyd, though nominally in charge, contributed little.

The NRU building was situated between NRX and the river, so that the windows looking on the river gave an uninterrupted view of the spectacular cliffs on the Quebec shore. The narrowing of the river here brought the cliffs up close to the Ontario shore. These windows, running almost the full height of the building, gave the reactor hall the appearance of a cathedral, within which the reactor took up a commanding central position.

The cliffs upon which the windows looked housed a family of ravens, the location of whose nest was visible to the naked eye. Over the years these large black birds had produced their own version of the famous cliffs of Dover. They stayed through the bitterest winter and became the plant's first harbingers of spring. In late February they would greet the growing warmth of the sun with croaks and hoarse shrieks of joy while outdoing each other in aerial acrobatics high over the plant.

———

Not only was NRU to be cooled with heavy water, but the design permitted the removal of individual fuel elements and their replacement with fresh fuel while the reactor ran at full power. This "on-power" fueling would be necessary if the plutonium produced was to be extracted efficiently. The reactor power was to be 200 megawatts.

It took six years of design and development and construction to bring NRU to the point of start-up: six years in which reputations were made or broken, six years of endless meetings held within AECL and between AECL and contractors, innumerable trips to Toronto, Ottawa, Montreal, and beyond, reports written and rewritten, papers read to scientific and technical societies, visitors entertained and conducted on tours, doubtful ministers placated, but – significantly – six years without comment or criticism from the Canadian public. The enthusiasm of AECL scientists and engineers had yet to be restrained by public criticism. This was to come in the generation that brought Allen Ginsberg and the "flower children" to prominence.

NRU became divergent at 6:10 a.m. on 3 November 1957, about the same time that NRX had become divergent ten years earlier. Its high neutron flux (four times that of NRX) and its extreme flexibility made it the world's most important research and development reactor. Heavy water leaks were a problem, but the leaks were located and closed one by one. A heavy water recovery system collected any leakage as well as heavy water vapour and thus prevented losses from becoming prohibitive. On-power removal and replacement of fuel also proved to be tricky, with at least one accident causing contamination and a delay for clean-up of the beautiful new NRU building. However, the problems were gradually solved, and in due course, irradiated fuel containing its maximum complement of plutonium was being shipped to the United States in large containers with thick walls of lead to absorb the penetrating radiation. These were drawn on flatbed trailers of tremendous carrying capacity. Transportation was overland by the existing highway system. Though the routes were cleared through official channels, there was no public protest. Indeed, there was little public knowledge. The project was secret.

The contrast with the situation today could not be greater. Canada's 1999 offer to test the destruction of weapons grade plutonium from the U.S. and Russian bomb programs by using it as fuel in Canadian reactors raised a storm of protest from a well-organized network of anti-nuclear activists in Canada and the United States. The practical and symbolic significance of this momentous development in international affairs appears to have been lost on them. For the very first time since the onset of the Cold War it was proposed internationally that fissionable material produced for nuclear explosives be permanently destroyed and, in the process, used to generate useful energy.

Yet these dedicated opponents of atomic energy will have none of it. It is not the use of plutonium in Canadian reactors that is at issue. All Canadian reactors produce plutonium from the effect of neutrons on the uranium fuel and obtain considerable useful energy from the fraction of plutonium that is fissile. What is at issue are the ancillary problems of safety and security in the shipment of large amounts of plutonium from Russia and the U.S. Canadian critics of the proposal range from university scientists to a variety of grassroots organizations. There were impassioned presentations to parliamentary committees in Ottawa and massive blockades of international routes such as the international bridge at Ogdensburg. Opposition at the end of 2001 was so intense to the first, symbolic shipment of 120 grams of plutonium (about the size of a thick lead pencil) that it was decided to fly the shipment clandestinely by private aircraft from the U.S. border to Chalk River.

————.

Who are these protestors and do they have just cause for protesting? The answers to both of these questions are not simple. The protestors come from all walks of life. What they share is a deep-seated aversion to the use of atomic energy coupled with a profound distrust of the authorities responsible for its development and use. In the United States, the origins of this distrust may be traced to the early years of the Cold War, when Russia and the U.S. were each attempting to outdo the other in the development of nuclear weapons. In that climate of undeclared war, arbitrary actions were justified as being in the best interests of the respective countries, without what in peacetime would be considered due process. Thus both countries engaged unrestrainedly in nuclear test explosions, showering poisonous radioactive material into the atmosphere. Bill Grummitt, director of the extreme low level radioactivity laboratory in Deep River, told me that he had to obtain powdered milk made before Hiroshima to find milk that was absolutely free from traces of radioactive strontium. This speaks both for the pervasiveness of the contamination from nuclear explosions in the atmosphere and for the incredible sensitivity of Grummitt's techniques.

Public reaction in Russia may have been muted by a political system that gave little or no heed to public concerns. The political system in the United States was far more responsive. Led by Linus Pauling, a distinguished winner of a Nobel Prize in chemistry, public concern in the U.S. was whipped up to the point where positive international action was eventually taken and a ban on atmospheric testing of nuclear weapons was signed both by the U.S. and the U.S.S.R.

It is an indication of the extent to which the nuclear establishment in the U.S. was bruised during these developments that Pauling lost his tenured position at the California Institute of Technology because of his public activities. In 1962 he was awarded the Nobel Peace Prize for his efforts, and became the only person to have been awarded two, unshared Nobel Prizes.

Pauling's achievement appeared to have been a signal to others with reservations about the U.S. nuclear program. It was a time of reaction against the accumulated tensions of the Cold War, in which families had been encouraged to build shelters that they could live in for days or weeks to protect themselves from the effects of atomic explosions; in which school children were drilled to take shelter under their desks upon a command from the teacher; and in which directions to public fall-out shelters had become a feature of urban landscapes. It is small wonder that a generation grew up bitterly opposed to the idea of war and anything connected with war. "Make love, not war!" was their cry, and they carried this motto to extremes previously unheard of. They were known as the flower children of the sixties and seventies and found their voice in the songs of Joan Baez and the poems of Allen Ginsberg. It became fashionable among intellectuals of a certain sort to challenge the authority of established institutions such as universities, public utilities, and local governments. The U.S. Atomic Energy Commission was a natural target. What had been considered inviolate policy in the years just after the war became fair game for critics and dissenters. This situation was made to order for the popular press, which thrived on the resulting conflict and made sure that each dissenting voice was heard prominently regardless of the dissenter's qualifications and even if the body of the news report gave scant or doubtful support to the dissenter.

As so often happens, activities in the United States spilled over into Canada. With the influx of American draft-dodgers during the Vietnam War, may of them strongly anti-nuclear, this became literally the case. This is not to say that Canadian scientists were insensitive to the fact that atomic energy had its dark side. Its first use, after all, had been as a weapon of devastating power. The dread of nuclear weapons, particularly at the height of the Cold War, hung like a dark cloud over all humanity; who could be more aware of this than the scientists? Some in Canada took refuge in the fact that this country had adopted a course of peaceful development of the atom, though the future explosion of an atomic device by India was to undermine even this favourable view of the situation.

As it was, scientists and engineers of AECL, who had become accustomed to being looked upon as the heroes of a new age, were quite unprepared for the initial onslaught of criticism. It is perhaps understandable that the reaction of many was to dismiss the critics as "kooks" and "wierdos." But this attitude became untenable as it became clear that many of the critics were not only men and women of unquestioned intelligence but in some cases individuals with advanced technical and scientific training.

Canadian nuclear scientists and engineers found themselves faced with the task not only of explaining to the general public what they were doing but of justifying it. Most were at a loss. Few were accustomed to speaking of their work in non-technical terms and fewer by far were able to articulate their deepest beliefs to an antagonistic audience. Most were treading on quicksand when dealing with the public, liable to be compromised by the slightest unfortunate turn of expression. One never knew what would be effective in influencing public opinion and what would not. I remember one public debate in the autumn of 1975 on the steps of the entrance to Carleton University in Ottawa when Ted Thexton, a bright and appealing young AECL engineer, won the evening when he said, "I raised my three children a couple of miles down wind from the reactor at Whiteshell." That sank in.

The reaction of individual scientists and engineers to this change in public acceptance of their work varied from one person to another. Most carried on with the work at hand, leaving the questions raised by the critics to others. Many felt that the criticism was ill-founded and needed only to have the situation made clear to the critics. Some reacted with impatience and even anger. Others considered argument hopeless. After a session with Prof. Gordon Edwards, a prominent critic, Howard Newcombe, a distinguished geneticist at Chalk River, said to me, "The man's a mystic. You can't reason with mysticism!" The situation was perhaps best described in the words of Cesare Marchetti, the Italian scientist: "Nuclear scientists have been too preoccupied with physics, to the neglect of metaphysics."

The corporate reaction to public criticism was to put strict control on information going out to the public and more effort into formal public relations both at AECL and Ontario Hydro, the two organizations deeply involved in atomic power development. The degree to which this was effective is hard to measure. To the committed anti-nuclear critic, any output from a public relations office was suspect, and the glossier and more seductive it was, the more suspect. To the general public these public relations communications may have been more appealing. Many were very well put together, and care was taken to insure they were scrupulously accurate: it had been learned that critics would pounce on any doubtful fact and run with the news to the ever-hungry popular press. As one science reporter put it, Canada's atomic energy program had been thrown into the "bull-ring of public opinion." It has been there ever since.

Neither AECL nor Ontario Hydro could ever assume again that their plans would have automatic public approval, and the cost in time and effort of dealing with the public had to be factored into the cost of future developments in atomic energy. When, as has happened, irresolute governing bodies were swayed by circumstances in which public antipathy was a factor, costs mounted astronomically and resulted in considerable public debt. This debt is very likely regarded by confirmed critics as the legacy of developing power from the atom.

6

Nuclear Power

"Now the moral of my story is not far.
If you ever want to buy an atom car,
You must really take a lease on an everlasting peace;
Never use this Energy for war!"
                    The Deep River Song

If the prospect of an atomic-powered vessel on the Ottawa was a distant one in the 1940s, the prospect of boating on the river was not. It had not been long before the inhabitants of Deep River of those early days took to the water in all kinds of craft. Led by sailing enthusiasts, Yacht Club members collaborated in building a fleet of Y-flyers, plywood hulls in the approximate shape of an aircraft wing in cross section and capable of great speed. Driven by a Marconi rig of sails and with a crew of two, the flyers would rise out of the water and plane along in a stiff following wind. A regular series of races was held during the boating season. The Ottawa is so wide at Deep River that respectable courses of a mile in each leg could be laid out. The prevailing wind was downstream and could be steady for hours at a time. At other times the breezes were fickle and changeable and posed a real challenge to sailors. The better sailors gained in time a knowledge of the river as intimate as that gained by anyone in its history. At still other times terrible winds would travel down the river, following the cliffs on the Quebec shore. These could be seen coming miles up the river. The only recourse was to strike the sails and ride out the gale, which never lasted more than fifteen minutes. The wind could be so strong, however, that the entire fleet would be carried far down the river, planing under bare poles.

In due course an elegant club house was built by the members under the great white pines that had once sheltered the Indian cabins. One of the cabins was kept for storage and as a memento of a past era. In time, national Y-flyer championships were held at Deep River, occasionally to be won by local members. A friendly match was held in the 1950s with visitors from the U.S. atomic project at Savannah River. The Americans, who were thoroughly trounced, mentioned that they could sail only part of the year because for six months the "water was very dirty." Alec Cruickshank, the chemist who had installed the beautiful parquet floor of the club house, replied that at Deep River the water for six months of the year was "very hard."

W.B. Lewis, to his credit, bought a Y-flyer when it came on the market and sailed in the races when his schedule would permit. He could not, of course, compete with the dedication of the sailing enthusiasts who lived and breathed sailing. His participation in races was largely token. Some wag maintained that the only time he came in first over the line was when he was sailing the previous race. He had the reputation, however, of being a real Captain Bligh, and it was a brave man who would crew for him.

––––––––.

The Lewises were dedicated naturalists. W.B.'s Y-flyer was late entering one season because a red squirrel was found to be raising her family under the foredeck and could not be disturbed until the young ones had left the nest.

There were flying squirrels, too, on Beach Avenue. Nocturnal and shy, these beautiful little creatures could be glimpsed only occasionally by lamplight, gliding great distances among the tops of the pines along the avenue. Isoline Lewis, to her great regret, had never seen a flying squirrel other than in a photograph, and with her poor eyesight had little hope of seeing one. She must have felt that it was a special dispensation the day she found, to her surprise and delight, a flying squirrel curled up in the pocket of an apron she had left on the clothesline overnight.

This naturalist interest could, at times, lead to unusual situations when the Lewises were entertaining. Lewis was proud of his homemade high fidelity record player and once entertained a room full of distinguished scientists from Europe and the United States by playing a recording of frog mating calls in the forests of the Amazon. It says a great deal for the self-control of some humans that the party was able to endure several minutes of these peculiar, indescribable noises without collapsing in laughter.

Isoline Lewis always maintained that her son had unusually keen sight. His brother, Jack, in England, was apparently gifted with second sight and, according to Mrs Lewis, even as a child saw and spoke to people that others could not see. According to friends of the family in England, Jack was as brilliant as his brother. W.B. was a devoted son and preparation for any one of his many trips away from Deep River always included filling a pin-cushion with needles he had threaded for his mother, whose eyesight was failing badly.

In the mid-fifties and early sixties, during the construction of a Nuclear Power Demonstration reactor further upstream on the Ottawa, teams of AECL engineers and scientists traveled for regular monthly meetings with the contractor, Canadian General Electric, in Peterborough, Ontario. The trips were made in an AECL eleven-passenger limousine, known unaffectionately as "The Snake," leaving Deep River at 7 a.m. and arriving in Peterborough at 11, in time for a meeting of about one hour before lunch. Meetings were continued after lunch until about 4 p.m., when the return journey was made. The trips were bad enough in the summer, but in winter they were truly dreadful. Willy Wilson, an experienced nuclear engineer, was once heard to moan, "My God, there must be an easier way to earn a living!"

There was one miserable winter morning when snow was sweeping over the Petawawa plains. Members of our team were picked up in sequence at our homes in Deep River. I got a seat midway along the "Snake" and Lewis, out of deference to seniority, was picked up last. This meant that W.B. had the last seat at the back of the limousine. As the car went past Petawawa, a bird flashed up out of the snow into the headlights and swept over the windshield. "Jesus, what was that?" exclaimed Wilson in the front seat beside the driver. "Pine grosbeak," answered Lewis from the rear of the limousine, and he was very probably right.

On the way home in the evening the party would generally stop for dinner in Bancroft or Barry's Bay. Lewis, out of deference, was always invited to order first. This meant that the others had to eat quickly when their order came, for Lewis did not like to linger over a meal and would depart for the "Snake" as soon as he was finished. This would signal a general departure, leaving many meals unfinished, a practice that did not win him many friends among his team.

———

The Nuclear Power Demonstration reactor (NPD) was Canada's first step into the development of useful power from the atom. This was a natural uranium/heavy water reactor designed to produce electricity. The project was to be a joint effort by AECL, Canadian General Electric (CGE), and Ontario Hydro, the provincial utility. CGE was to design the nuclear portion and construct the station. AECL was to pay for the nuclear portion. Ontario Hydro was to design and pay for the conventional portion and commission and operate the station. CGE had bought into the arrangement by setting up a new department, Civilian Atomic Power Department, CAPD, at its Peterborough plant and had contributed $2 million toward the cost of design and engineering development.

AECL, in its participation, was fulfilling the mandate set forth in its April 1952 letters patent to "develop the peaceful uses of Atomic Energy for the benefit of all Canadians." If the production of plutonium in the NRU reactor for the U.S. nuclear weapons program had hardly fitted into this objective, it was justified by its paying for that reactor's costly design and development. The wartime partnership of Canada, the U.S., and Britain had created close ties, both professional and political, among the three countries that persisted well into the fifties, and by 1952 the Cold War was in full swing, profoundly affecting decisions such as the provision of plutonium to the United States. In any case, plutonium production was only one of the capabilities of the NRU, which had become a tremendous asset both for research and development and for the production of isotopes.

C.D. Howe, as minister of Trade and Commerce, announced on 24 March 1955 that Canada would proceed with the design and construction of the Nuclear Power Demonstration reactor at a site on the Ottawa upstream from Deep River and about two miles below the Rapides des Joachims, which had been dammed by Ontario Hydro for their large hydroelectric project at Rolphton.

The sod-turning ceremony at the NPD site was held on 19 September 1956 and was attended by Leslie M. Frost, the premier of Ontario, and Howe at one of his last public appearances. The controversial Pipeline Debate in which he was involved was soon to remove him and his well-loved prime minister, Louis St Laurent, from office. The sod for the shovels wielded by Howe and Frost was brought in for the occasion, as the site was largely sand and rock.

The logic for the decision to proceed with nuclear-electric generation lay in the fact that, with the completion of the St

Lawrence Seaway, the potential for hydroelectric power production in Ontario was nearly exhausted. Coal-fired power stations were then the alternative, but coal had to be imported from Pennsylvania, since the coal in the Maritimes was both far away and of the wrong quality, being too soft and too full of sulfur. Canada had even then vast stores of uranium (and much more has since been discovered in Saskatchewan). It was logical to develop this source of power. The argument at the time was purely economic. The question of the pollution caused by coal-fired stations and the drastic effects of carbon dioxide in the atmosphere on global warming would be raised many years later.

———

AECL's area of expertise dictated that NPD should be a natural uranium/heavy water reactor. A serious critic of this route to atomic power turned out to be Winnett Boyd, who had been the chief engineer for the C.D. Howe Company for the construction of NRU. He argued that Canada was mistaken in its decision to stay with the heavy water design, which would limit steam temperatures to about 250 degrees Celsius. He proposed an advanced reactor concept using graphite in place of the heavy water and a helium gas coolant operating at 500 degrees Celsius or even higher, an arrangement that would give far higher thermal efficiency of operation. He was right about the efficiency, but to switch to an advanced reactor of this type meant starting out all over again. Boyd was handsome, a man of expensive tastes with a shock of prematurely white hair over dark eyebrows. He argued his case persuasively in the press and on television. His adversary defending the AECL position was J. Lorne Gray, a later president of AECL who was then general manager. Gray's persona and delivery were no match for Boyd, but his arguments prevailed. Boyd seriously lacked credibility in the eyes of AECL, the federal government, and Ontario Hydro.

———————.

Experience with the design of NRU, both moderated and cooled with heavy water, led inexorably to the conclusion that NPD should be similarly moderated and cooled with heavy water if the full benefit of the natural uranium fuel was to be obtained. However, NPD would pose fresh challenges. NRU had heavy water pumped in circuits not much above room temperature; NPD required heavy water to be pumped in circuits at 300 degrees Celsius and 100 atm pressure. If leakage had been a problem in NRU, it promised to be a problem of a much greater magnitude in NPD. The design of joints and pump seals became another part of AECL expertise, so much so that when, many years later, the fatal accident with the NASA space shuttle *Challenger* occurred, AECL became the prime consultant on the fuel seal that failed, and NASA eventually adopted a design for the seal proposed by AECL.

The fuel for this new Nuclear Power Demonstration had also to be developed. The three earlier reactors, ZEEP, NRX, and NRU, were fueled with uranium sheathed in aluminum. Aluminum could not be used in water at 300 degrees, a temperature much higher than that experienced by aluminum in kettles and cooking vessels. Zircaloy-2, the alloy of zirconium developed by Westinghouse, could be used, but the techniques of forming and welding Zircaloy for fuel sheathing had to be developed and reliable producers of the alloy had to be trained. Aluminum could be used for the heavy water tank, for the heavy water temperature would be only slightly above room temperature, but Zircaloy would have to be used for the tubes containing the fuel, for the surface temperature would be in the neighbourhood of 300 degrees Finally, the fuel itself could not be uranium metal, for this tended to expand and distort at high temperatures and in an intense neutron flux. After years of testing and development, the fuel chosen consisted of pellets of uranium oxide sintered at high temperature into a dense ceramic. The pellets were loaded into tubes of Zircaloy-2 by hand and the tubes then welded shut.

The step from the design on paper of a reactor to its actual construction is very large, and one often overlooked by those recording the progress of nuclear power. To achieve a functioning reactor, members of the AECL project at Chalk River became expert in pump and joint seals, zirconium metallurgy, forming and welding, high temperature ceramics, nuclear fuel fabrication and testing, water chemistry, and a host of other trades and sciences. Armed with the experience in loop operation in NRX and NRU and advanced skills in the handling and examination of highly radioactive materials, AECL led the world in the development of fuel for atomic power reactors.

My involvement was in the chemistry of many of the tests of prototype fuel in loops in NRX and NRU. This involved sampling and analysis of the cooling water in the loop at all hours of the day and night. I used to enjoy the occasional night shift, when the whole plant would be in darkness except for the street lights and lights in the major buildings, and everything was so quiet that one heard clearly the ventilation fans in each building as one walked by. Deer were often seen on the road to and from the plant on these occasions.

As a comment on the manpower available at Chalk River relative to that in the United States, it was the usual practice at AECL for development problems to be tackled by a lone professional (often young) aided by one or two technicians, whereas the team in the U.S. was much larger, almost by a factor of ten. Thus junior Canadian technical officers found themselves talking to division heads in the United States, and often discovered that they knew more, by virtue of hands-on experience, than their American opposite numbers. Nevertheless, American technology had a leadership role. What the Americans were doing weighed heavily with AECL management as well as with our political masters. I can remember the exasperation and despair at Chalk River when it was decided in the United States that the first fuel charge for their Dresden reactor would be sheathed in stainless steel. Some American experiments had shown that Zircaloy-2 became brittle when exposed to water at 300 degrees Celsius. The vision of a brittle Zircaloy sheath cracking and releasing hideously radioactive fission products into the coolant stream was a nightmare scenario. The Americans could overcome the neutron absorption by the stainless steel by enriching the uranium oxide with U-235 from their weapons program. Of course, we could not, so we were faced with the problem of determining *why* Zircaloy-2 became brittle. It took us a couple of years, but we found out, and were able to stay on the course with Zircaloy-2. Now we know a great deal about zirconium alloys in high temperature water.

———

The design of NPD was not straightforward. Following the lead given by the earlier reactors, the first concept was of a pressure vessel of heavy water in which fuel elements would be suspended vertically in their respective cooling channels. The vessel was in an advanced stage of fabrication when the decision was made to change the design drastically so that the fuel channels would run horizontally through a tank of heavy water. There were excellent reasons for this, but it meant canceling the original contract, which involved an expense in the millions of dollars, and starting on a new one. Recall that this decision was made in cautious, conservative Canada and reflect on the courage demanded by nuclear development!

The new design opened all kinds of possibilities. Now the reactor presented two faces, one into which the fuel could be fed and one from which the spent fuel could be extracted. Furthermore, the fuel would rest in the coolant channel and not have to be suspended. In fact it could be pushed along as

The first fueling machine built for the NPD reactor, 1963. This posed photograph shows one face of the reactor in its subterranean chamber. No human being would be near the reactor during operation. The end-fittings and end-plugs for each fuel channel indicate a grid pattern of channels designed to maximize the effectiveness of neutrons from fission in sustaining the nuclear reaction. The fueling machine is lowered into the chamber on its stalk. Its partner is lowered simultaneously into the chamber at the other face of the reactor. The two must then attach themselves to either end of the same channel, remove the end-plugs and feed or receive fuel as required, then replace the end-plugs and proceed to the next operation, all done under remote control from a control room far above in another part of the station. That the machines should work at all is a wonder. That they should work repeatedly over long periods of time is beyond belief. In fact, the machines were a source of problems during the first year or so of NPD operation, but the problems were solved with determination and ingenuity. Photo No. C5253, Canadian General Electric, Peterborough.

A 1964 photograph of the Nuclear Power Demonstration generating station in operation. The part of the building nearest the camera houses the administration offices. Next come the control room and fueling-machine bays. The large rectangular building is the turbine hall. The reactor is in an underground vault. The camera is looking downriver in the direction of Deep River, which is far down the river and out of sight. The booms used to guide the rafts of logs in the river are seen anchored to rock-filled cribs spaced along the edge of the shallows. The juxtaposition of old and new is intriguing. NPD operated successfully for twenty-five years, putting power into the Ontario Hydro grid and serving as a test bed for development and a training ground for nuclear staff. It demonstrated conclusively the feasibility of the CANDU concept. AECL Photo No. 7611-2826-21 new fuel was added and then moved out the other end of the channel. If machines could be made to do this automatically, the reactor could be refueled on-power, that is, without shutting down. This would be a great advantage in a power-generating reactor, since there would be no interruption of power.

If these considerations appear complex to the reader, they were even more complex to those who had to design the reactor's components. Perhaps the most complex components were the fueling machines, which were designed by CGE. These machines operated simultaneously at each face of the reactor, one automatically opening the coolant channel at 300 degrees Celsius and 100 atm pressure, inserting a new fuel element, then closing the channel, while the other simultaneously received the spent fuel pushed out of the channel, then closed its end in turn. That these devices worked at all was miraculous. That they should work repeatedly over long periods of time seemed beyond belief. In fact, problems with the fueling machines plagued the design, but, as with other design and operational problems, they were eventually solved.

———

NPD was completed in 1962 and set a world record immediately upon start-up. Earlier nuclear power stations in the U.S. and Britain had required many weeks of gradual stepping up to full power with tests and adjustments every step of the way. NPD went from zero to twenty megawatts electrical at full power in less than a month, a success reflecting the thoroughness of the CGE design, as well as the abilities of Lorne McConnell, the Hydro supervisor in charge. NPD had already been publicized by the *Pembroke Observer* of 7 June 1958 with a detailed, half-tone diagram of the station in cross-section that occupied most of the upper half of the front page. It can be assumed that not many of the paper's readers noticed or appreciated the fact that the diagram was upside down, though close examination would have shown two visitors to the station with their feet apparently on a ceiling of the structure.

————.

NPD was operated under the supervision of Ontario Hydro, putting electric power into the Hydro grid. It served for twenty-five years as a power station, a training ground for future power reactor operators, and also as a test bed for future power reactors. NPD demonstrated conclusively that heavy water could be handled at high temperature and pressure and that losses would not be prohibitive, owing to heavy water recovery techniques. Admiral Rickover's characterization of the Canadian concept as a "reactor of a thousand leaks" was a memorable put-down, nothing more.

————.

NPD was, in a sense, the Canadian program's last direct connection with the Ottawa River. Deep River had become a burgeoning community in its own right, serving the AECL and Hydro populations, as well as surrounding, smaller communities. The Chalk River Nuclear Laboratories would remain a centre of excellence, not only in the field of atomic energy but in many areas of research and development. Ontario Hydro's nuclear power plant program would always lean heavily on this concentration of expertise. However, with the completion of NPD and its successful operation, AECL's sights were raised to other parts of Ontario and even abroad.

NPD represented a point of departure for Canadian General Electric as well. The team assembled in its Civilian Atomic Power Department in Peterborough was first class, as was evidenced by the work it had done on NPD. The problem for CAPD was to break into the nuclear power market in Canada and abroad. As far as Canada was concerned, CAPD laboured under a serious handicap. It was a branch operation of General Electric in the United States and directives came from head office in Schenectady, New York. Excellent though the team might be, it was constrained to follow head office guidelines. As an example, to make progress in the nuclear market CAPD would have to collaborate closely with the Canadian government at the federal level, since departments of government like the Atomic Energy Control Board, Export Credit Insurance Corporation, and Industry, Trade and Commerce, to name a few, did not appreciate being kept in the dark and had considerable influence on negotiations at home and abroad. Head office, Schenectady, strongly discouraged involvement with government departments. This meant that potential contracts worth many millions of dollars could only be discussed informally with government contacts.

In seeking to make sales in the export market – "offshore" in CGE parlance – the Canadian company was further constrained by the Co-Com list, an American list of countries with which American companies could not do business. CGE could not operate, therefore, as a Canadian company. Even where sales were permitted, head office stipulated the terms of contracts. Thus, when the American parent company had repeatedly lost money on nuclear "turn-key" contracts, contracts in which the company provided complete plants in every detail and then handed the key to the customer, it issued a company-wide directive forbidding turn-key proposals. J. Herbert Smith, president of CGE, was required by Schenectady to forbid turn-key proposals on the part of CAPD, although the Canadian company had never lost money in this way and turn-key plants were especially attractive to first-time customers for nuclear power.

CAPD had to struggle on all fronts, as much against its senior management as against unsympathetic departments in the Canadian government and against competitors in the nuclear power market. Ottawa, it must be noted, recognized the excellence of the team at CGE, and cast about for ways to keep it together. Pakistan had complained bitterly of the preferential aid being given by Canada to India in atomic energy. I represented AECL at a number of interdepartmental meetings in Ottawa to finance a nuclear-electric generating station for Pakistan under very favourable terms and to give the contract to CGE. It was in 1966, in the wake of this development, that I transferred to CGE. I was mistakenly credited with the Pakistan contract and welcomed accordingly. CAPD took on a new life and proceeded with the successful design and construction of KANUPP, a 130-megawatt natural uranium/heavy water nuclear-electric generating station for Karachi in Pakistan.

Inaugurated on 23 November 1972 by President Zulfikar Ali Bhutto, this was the first Canadian nuclear power station to be constructed abroad and its success confirmed not only the Canadian reactor concept but also the excellent capability of the CGE team. Today it is the oldest CANDU station in operation anywhere. It was clear, however, that opportunities for CGE would always be limited because of the distrust felt in Ottawa of a company dominated by American interests. The team's efforts to obtain other contracts abroad in Argentina, Finland, and Romania, including its brilliant VENTURE program (in which nuclear engineers from eleven countries were brought to Peterborough to collaborate on the design of a Canadian reactor) were crippled by this circumstance.

At home in Canada, Ontario Hydro's refusal to deal with CGE as a nuclear power plant designer was the deciding factor. Conventional commercial wisdom of the fifties and sixties had it that a business could not be developed on the export market alone. These circumstances forced the company to withdraw from the field in 1968. CAPD was shut down, with the exception of its profitable nuclear fuel fabrication and fuel handling (fueling machines) departments, and the team of engineers was largely absorbed by other departments of the company, by universities, and by Ontario Hydro, which was building nuclear capability and embarking on a serious program of nuclear power plant building.

––––––––.

It was at this point that the headmaster of a small private boys' school in Lakefield invited me to join the school as a science master. Kate and I were intrigued, as we had no children of our own. I decided to try it in spite of dire negative views of colleagues at Canadian General Electric. I had the feeling that I might contribute something to the school from my experience in "Big Science" and in government affairs. What a laugh! I soon found that when the schoolmaster closes the classroom door on himself and ten or twenty boys, the situation is immediately reduced to first principles in the interactions between human beings. I learned more about myself during those subsequent years of teaching than at any other time in my life. I returned to AECL head office after seven years as a schoolmaster, a wiser and, I hope, a better person.

––––––––.

Although a critical review of the AECL development program might question at times whether effort was always exerted "for the benefit of all Canadians," there is justification in the fact that every step of the program led toward the very efficient nuclear-electric generating system known as CANDU. If CGE was gradually squeezed out of the partnership it had had with AECL and Ontario Hydro in the NPD project, a very close working relationship developed between AECL and Hydro in future atomic projects.

Ontario Hydro's chief engineer, Harold Smith, had been seconded to Chalk River to lead a team of engineers from AECL, Hydro, and other engineering firms, notably Montreal Engineering, which had seconded John Foster, Smith's deputy in the team. It is Foster who is credited with the acronym CANDU, for "Canadian Deuterium Uranium." The group went by the title Nuclear Power Plant Division and had the task of design-

TAKING PHOTOGRAPHS IN FAST WATER AT 300° CELSIUS
AND A HUNDRED ATMOSPHERES PRESSURE, CA 1960.

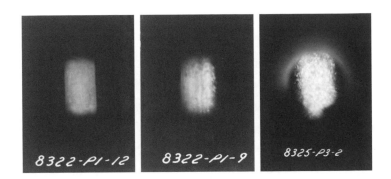

These apparently insignificant photographs represent a major technical achievement, the determination of the point at which water ceases to flow smoothly over the surface of a cylindrical fuel element operating at power reactor conditions and starts to boil, thus losing its heat transfer efficiency. The camera is peering through a circular window specially constructed to stand the pressure in the fuel channel and resist etching by the water at this elevated temperature. The photographs were taken with a very fast flash in order to catch the start of boiling, the illumination coming through a second window at an angle from the first. The fuel element is not real, of course, but a dummy constructed to reproduce the conditions in an actual fuel element. This involved getting 75,000 watts of heat into a Zircaloy tube three-quarters of an inch in diameter and two feet long. The manufacturers of electric heaters thought the project was impossibly mad. It was achieved, though, by making up special heaters of platinum, which not only stood up to the temperature but gave a means of measuring it. Hundreds of pictures were taken with a polaroid camera in order to adjust the experiment to the proper conditions for measurement. Courtesy of Ralph S. Flemons, CAPD, CGE.

ing a large nuclear electric plant based on the heavy water reactor. The design that emerged was for a station of 200 megawatts electrical capacity.

———.

Ontario Hydro, as a provincial utility charged with supplying electricity to customers in Ontario at cost, was interested in the promise of generating electricity from Canadian uranium more cheaply than it could be generated from Pennsylvania coal. Electricity cost comparisons between nuclear and coal-fired stations had been a preoccupation at Chalk River ever since the decision to proceed with the CANDU concept. Every development in CANDU design, the configuration of fuel, the thickness of metal parts and their contribution to neutron loss, cost of heavy water, amortization of plant and materials, etc., was weighed against the effect it would have on the final cost of electrical power from CANDU plants. AECL kept a "fever chart" of costs as an indication of progress in bringing costs down. W.B. Lewis played a major part in all of this, issuing report after report by his own hand and exerting his considerable influence on staff members whom he found to be useful. He had no compunctions about asking them to work at all hours and over weekends. After all, he did it himself. If any one person can be said to have fathered the Canadian Deuterium Uranium reactor, it is W.B. He was made a Companion of the Order of Canada for his work.

———.

In the meantime, a new president had taken over the direction of AECL. J. Lorne Gray had come to the Chalk River Project in 1950 from the National Research Council in Ottawa after a distinguished career during the war in the RCAF, from which he had retired with the rank of wing commander. The man he replaced was not Dr Mackenzie but W.J. Bennett, who had taken over from Mackenzie at the behest of his mentor, C.D. Howe, shortly after AECL was established as a crown corporation. Bennett was neither a scientist nor an engineer but "one of Howe's boys," who had worked closely with the great man during the war and had his complete confidence. Bennett made almost no impact on the community in Deep River. He was no more than an occasional visitor, but as an Ottawa insider he had influenced crucial decisions as to the nature of the corporation and the direction it should take.

If W.B. Lewis could be likened by some critics to an English "carpetbagger" on the Canadian scene (he had in fact become a staunch Canadian), Lorne Gray was the ultimate local boy, a Junior A hockey player and graduate in engineering from the University of Saskatchewan. When AECL was established, Gray became its general manager. From this it was a short step to vice-president of administration and thence in 1958 to president when Bennett retired to go into the private sector. Lewis continued on in Chalk River as vice president of research and development; the idea of turning him loose in Ottawa had given the directors of the company the shivers. Gray, however, lost no time in settling into the head office in Ottawa, which soon took on his personality. He swam easily in the political currents of that city, thanks to experience and contacts made during the war and during his tenure at NRC. He understood clearly how federal government decisions were made and what was needed to influence them. He moved in the right circles, knew the right people, and played an excellent game of golf. The beautiful fieldstone fireplace of the Deep River Golf Club attests to his skill as a mason as well as his love of the game. Within AECL he had qualities of leadership that inspired friendship as well as respect. I once said to him, during an after-hours drink of scotch in his office, that I would rather "go down in flames with him" than "win" with someone else. I did not know then how prophetic that statement might be.

Gray was at home in the Ottawa cocktail circuit. His monthly luncheon parties at Henri Berger's (pronounced "Burger's") were a "must do" for the movers and shakers in the government, as were his Wednesday afternoon rounds of golf. These functions were by no means purely entertainment. They were opportunities to bring important officials like Ed Ritchie of External Affairs and Bob Bryce of Finance up to date with developments in the nuclear field – so remote from common understanding – and to explain AECL's strategies for keeping abreast of them.

It was a time when the fortunes of AECL were at a peak. With Lewis at Chalk River and Gray in Ottawa, a board of directors that included the heads of provincial utilities as well as powerful individuals in business and government, AECL flourished, often to the exasperation and envy of other organizations competing for research and development funding.

The decision to build a 200-megawatt power reactor at Douglas Point on Lake Huron had the backing of Ottawa and the government of Ontario. Ontario Hydro was to operate the station in its power grid. The design had been produced by AECL's Nuclear Power Plant Division (NPPD), which was to provide project management. This was AECL's first venture away from the Ottawa River and the first large-scale project for NPPD. Staff there were augmented with engineers from Ontario Hydro and private industry. Gordon Churchill, the minister then responsible for AECL, announced on 18 June 1959 the decision of Cabinet to proceed with the CANDU reactor.

AECL had to struggle to achieve its objective. Rather than separating the design into major blocks and contracting with suppliers to furnish a whole block – for example, the steam generating system and turbine – the station was broken down into about 400 separate items, with different contracts furnishing each item. Ontario Hydro preferred to work this way to obtain competition among different suppliers (this is also why it refused to deal with CGE as a power plant designer). The result in this case, however, was chaos. Even with the best of controls and intentions, the interfaces between items supplied by one supplier and another often did not match up. For example, CGE had obtained the contract for the pressure tube end-fittings but not for the plugs to close the pressure tubes. These were supplied by a company in England, and although they were manufactured to tight specifications, they did not work and had to be re-machined by CGE. The inspection and approval of drawings became a nightmare and the construction time began to trail off into the future. Visitors to Douglas Point during this period would at times see a length of pipe lying in a trench, waiting for drawings to show how and where it was to be connected.

Though the delay in completion was largely due to Hydro's contracting preferences, commissioning and start-up were Hydro successes. Douglas Point eventually came to power in 1967. After Douglas Point, Hydro relied largely upon its own design and construction people for CANDU stations. In this it was at first remarkably successful, for future stations at Pickering on Lake Ontario and Bruce on Lake Huron led the world in performance as nuclear-electric generators. In due course over 50 per cent of the electricity generated in Ontario was produced by CANDU stations using native uranium, and the low cost of electricity in Ontario was the envy of the world.

One cannot pass over the fact that from 1990 onward, these stations have shown declining performance, so much so that a team of American specialists was engaged at considerable expense in 1998 by the provincial government to analyse the situation, identify the problems, and bring the performance of the stations back to where it was. Their arrival was greeted with condescension by knowledgeable Canadians in the field ("They can't even spell CANDU!") but it represented the first serious study of the CANDU system by Americans. Carl Andognini, the American charged with nuclear matters, absolved the CANDU reactor immediately by reporting that the design was "robust." In testimony before the Senate Committee on Energy, Environment, and Natural Resources on 13 April 2000 he said, "I firmly believe that the CANDU technology you have in Canada is the safest nuclear technology in the world." The poor performance of the CANDU stations was traced to management problems, which had dogged Ontario Hydro for many years.

As a provincial public utility, Hydro was subject to decisions of the provincial government, which at one time replaced the commissioner with a board of directors who, though excellent people, had important responsibilities outside of Hydro and often had to leave crucial decisions to staff in the next echelon below. The appointments to the board were, of course, political, and this injected political uncertainty into the operation of the utility. The provincial government demanded staff cutbacks and thinning in financially lean years, apparently oblivious of the fact that the approved construction of new stations meant that increases in trained personnel would be required. Andognini had to shut down units at Pickering and Bruce in order to have enough trained personnel to run the remaining units properly.

The story is of sufficient importance to deserve a separate telling in another place. Suffice it to say that, since the appointment of a board of directors, Hydro had been the object of tinkering by successive provincial governments unwilling to reveal to consumers in Ontario the increasing cost of electricity. As new nuclear stations were built and brought on line to meet the projected demand for electricity, charges on capital borrowing should have been added in an orderly fashion to the cost of power. Instead, because of the reluctance of governments to raise the price to the consumer, the charges were allowed to accumulate in a provincial debt that ballooned year after year. This was a recipe for financial disaster.

The Progressive Conservative government of Mike Harris presumed to address this problem by privatizing Ontario Hydro and breaking it into a power generating company, Ontario Power Generation, which runs the nuclear stations, and a power distribution company, Hydro One Networks. The outcome of these measures is a matter for speculation. The current Liberal government of Dalton McGuinty has retreated from privatizing Hydro One. However, it is clear that the first objective of Ontario Power is to concentrate on returning the performance of its nuclear stations into the top category in the world.

AECL facilities and expertise at Chalk River were used by Hydro in past years in technical support of its program. This will undoubtedly be the case with Ontario Power Generation. What else the future holds for Chalk River is uncertain. Whether it will remain a centre of excellence in the fast-flowing stream of science and technology will depend upon its leaders and on the whims of Canadian governments. Whatever may happen, nothing can take from it the achievements of its halcyon days at the dawn of the nuclear age.

As a research and development centre Chalk River's success has been outstanding. The reasons for this and the lessons to be learned from the Chalk River experience have been studied and described with great clarity by J.A.L. "Archie" Robertson in the final chapter of *Canada Enters the Nuclear Age*, a work published in 1997 by McGill-Queen's University Press. A great deal of the work of CANDU development involved working with outside firms under contract with Chalk River. In this way nuclear expertise and nuclear quality manufacturing capability became widely diffused in Canadian industry. There is no need to recapitulate Archie's findings here, but to those of us who took part in the development of CANDU the advantages and effectiveness of the Chalk River methods appear obvious, and it is with sadness and disbelief that some of us have witnessed the "contracting out" procedures of government departments in Ottawa and elsewhere.

If proof is needed of Canada's supremacy, one need only turn to the results summarized in table 21.1 of Archie's study.

Here the total nuclear R and D expenditures of different countries, in billions of U.S. dollars, are totalled up to the year 1985, that is, by the time the CANDU reactor had become well established as a successful nuclear power system. I have amplified on the information in the table with my own comments, which indicate the degree of success in developing a reactor suitable for generating power.

U.S.	$31.6 b	Two viable indigenous reactor types
France	12.2	Two viable indigenous reactor types
West Germany	11.2	No indigenous reactor types
Japan	9.6	No indigenous reactor types
U.K.	6.0	One viable indigenous reactor type
Italy	3.4	No indigenous reactor types
Canada	2.5	One viable indigenous reactor type

I have identified the reactor types as "viable" when they were used successfully over the long term. One might comment further and note that France, the former West Germany, and Japan have relied largely on the United States for supply of U.S.-developed nuclear power reactors. France and the U.K. have each developed a uniquely national concept, neither of which is likely to be competitive worldwide. France's "fast reactor" has also been considered "viable," though both France and the U.K. will probably rely on U.S. reactors in the future. Italy has one station supplied by Britain and one by the U.S. None of its indigenous R and D has led to material success in this field. AECL's knowledge, experience, and developmental techniques and the success they have brought in the field of nuclear power development speak for themselves in the data of this table.

———————

Kate and I left Deep River in 1965. Even by then it had changed dramatically from the original cluster of wartime fours and sixes housing 100 or so inhabitants. By 1956 the population was nearly 4,000 and in 1966 it peaked at just over 5,700. This expansion was due in part to the expansion at the plant and in part to natural increase. All those scientists and engineers who had arrived in their early thirties had started families, and for a while Deep River was said to have not only the highest number of Ph.D.'s per square mile in Canada but also the country's highest birthrate.

It was an unusually vibrant community. The government furnished it with outstanding facilities (sometimes to the envy of the surrounding towns of the Ottawa Valley), incomes were stable, there was no unemployment, and no housing shortages. The number of clubs belonging to the Community Association soared to over one hundred at one time, and the town was certainly the only one of its size in Canada to boast of a symphony orchestra and a cricket club. "Welcome to the Good Life" read the sign on the highway for visitors approaching from the east, though it was later amended by an enterprising teenager to "Welcome to the Half Life."

In the mid-eighties, however, cutbacks in government funding to AECL and other federal research centres in the area began to take their toll, and since then the town has been in decline. The population now hovers around 4,000, and a sizeable percentage of the inhabitants are at retirement age. The chief protagonists of the CANDU story long ago left the stage, and the laboratories at Chalk River have been carrying on with dwindling resources. Until recently it has looked as if Lew Kowarski's prophecies about the life of large research centres would come true. But, once again, changes appear to be in the wings. The success of the new CANDU stations in China has attracted the attention of the world, particularly the United States. The U.S. Department of Energy has recently authorized utilities in the U.S. to examinine the CANDU system as "one of only two viable nuclear power options" in the world today.

The U.S. Nuclear Regulatory Commission paid a visit to the Chalk River Laboratories and was pleasantly surprised by the technical and theoretical capabilities it found there. The potential market is such that Hitachi and SNC Lavalin, large private investors, are interested in investing in AECL, and the Canadian government is examining ways in which private investment might be made in a crown corporation. Bechtel, one of the largest construction companies in the world, collaborated in the construction of the Chinese stations, came away impressed with AECL project management skills, and has indicated its preference for bidding with AECL on future projects. The future for AECL and CANDU looks bright. What the future will bring to Deep River remains to be seen, but these are signs of possible renewal. Let us hope that a new day will dawn.

Epilogue

Nuclear Critics

*"... one kilogram (2.2 pounds) of matter, if converted entirely
into energy, would give 25 billion kilowatt hours of energy.
This is equal to the energy that would be generated by the
total electric power industry in the United States ... running
for approximately two months."*

The above statement is made in the first pages of *Atomic Energy
for Military Purposes*, the official history of the Manhattan Project, which was first published in July 1945 by Prof. Henry D.
Smyth, chairman of the Department of Physics of Princeton
University and consultant to the Manhattan Project. I wonder
how many of his readers grasped the awesome significance of
these statements. The figures refer to U.S. electrical capacity in
1939 but give the reader an inkling of the enormous energies
latent in matter. If one considers that a medium-size stick of
hardwood for the fireplace might weigh one kilogram and
considers the energy available from that stick of wood if all
the potential atomic energy could be used, one begins to appreciate that, in using this source of energy, one is entering a
domain never before part of the human experience. The figures
are astronomical and almost beyond comprehension. No
thinking person can fail to be impressed by the magnitudes
involved. It is no wonder that some have fears about the use
of atomic energy.

Engineers and scientists who have become accustomed to
working in this field may tend to put the magnitude of the
energies involved out of their conscious thoughts. In 1975,
John Foster, who had been head of AECL Power Projects, was
being groomed for the position of president of the crown cor-

poration. I was with him once when, railing against the negative attitudes of anti-nuclear critics of the AECL program, he
declared that he was "not afraid of atomic energy." By this time
public opposition to nuclear power was becoming vocal, and
ill-founded but effective criticism of AECL's program was growing even in Ottawa. I feared John would gain few brownie
points with the public with such a statement and pointed out
to him that he was indeed "afraid" of atomic energy and that he
designed around those fears. We were standing in front of the
elevators at the AECL Ottawa head office. Lorne Gray, the retir-
ing president, came up just then, overheard the discussion,
and interjected, "Yes, and you hope to God the design works!"

——————

That Canadians had tapped into this source of energy and
done it successfully and safely was surely an achievement to be
acknowledged. The credit goes to many, many Canadians, who
spent many thousands of hours of the most productive years
of their lives in testing ideas, solving technical problems, developing new materials and techniques, correcting errors, and
coping with unforeseen difficulties. In his last message to AECL
staff just before his retirement in 1975 Lorne Gray had this to say:

Through the years I have seen Canada's nuclear program grow from what
was little more than a research operation in a cluster of laboratories at Chalk
River to a major national enterprise reaching from coast to coast and involving governments, utilities, manufacturers, business firms, investment houses, universities and a very considerable number of people in a wide range of
occupations ... All credit is due to those who never lost faith in the program,
who stuck with it when times were hard and saw it through from setbacks to
success. I refer not only to those who were directly involved in the program
but also to governments that bore the ultimate responsibility. Without their
strong and consistent support the program would not be where it is today.

An entire industry has grown up in this country, employing
as many as 30,000 people, all of whom are involved in some

aspect of producing power from the atom. A whole new armoury of skills and capabilities has been developed and new standards of perfection established. There was nothing quite like this in Canada before, and one can speculate on how much of the current strength in high-tech industries owes something to the development of atomic energy.

.————.

In view of these achievements, it was particularly unfortunate that Lorne Gray's departure from the office of president was marred by political scandal and innuendo. The explosion of a nuclear device by India in 1974 had cast a pall upon Canada's atomic energy program, for the Indians had used the Canadian NRX-type reactor at Trombay furnished by AECL to produce the plutonium for the explosion. No matter that the reactor had been supplied in the late fifties under the Colombo Plan as an initiative of the Department of External Affairs in Ottawa. No matter that it had been supplied with assurances from Dr Homi Bhabha, director of the Indian Department of Atomic Energy and a friend and former colleague of Cockcroft and Lewis at Cambridge. No matter that the heavy water for the reactor had been supplied by the United States. And least of all did it matter that the Indian officials who had pushed for the explosion (after the death of Dr Bhabha in an air crash in 1966) assured everyone that the explosion was for "peaceful purposes." Canada, and in particular AECL, had been instrumental in the proliferation of nuclear weapons. This was a blow to the heart of AECL's program.

Lorne Gray, then sixty-two years of age, was hit particularly hard by this turn of events and was depressed by it. Whether it precipitated his early retirement is questionable; he had been suffering for some years with rheumatoid arthritis and it was getting worse every year. But I was puzzled and disturbed by the reaction of W.B. Lewis, whom I cornered at a seminar at Queen's University a couple of weeks after the Indian explosion. I knew how much we had done for the Indians to bring them into the nuclear age and I was furious at what I perceived to be their duplicity. I asked W.B. if he would be a signatory to an open letter to the Indians condemning their bad faith, and he said he would not. He gave no reason for this and left me with the feeling that he did not share my anger. He may have been under instructions to keep quiet, but I had expected some sympathy on his part. None was forthcoming.

AECL had taken over the CANDU export program from Canadian General Electric in 1969. Lorne Gray and Herb Smith had signed an agreement to that effect at the time CGE had withdrawn from nuclear power marketing. This had led AECL into an agreement to supply Argentina with a nuclear-electric generating station under contract terms that had been established by CGE. It should be stated here that CANDU stations do not resemble NRX reactors in any material way, and it is impractical to use a CANDU station to produce plutonium. Unfortunately, the Argentine contract had not made allowances for the runaway inflation being experienced in Argentina in 1975 and AECL stood to lose a considerable sum of money on the project.

A much more favourable contract was being concluded with the government of South Korea for a similar station. To win the contract AECL had employed an agent, an Israeli operator experienced on the international scene, and had paid him a fee (about 2 per cent of the contract price) conditional upon winning the contract for a plant at Wolsung in South Korea. This was a normal process in the world of international business, but there was revulsion in Ottawa at the thought of agent's fees being paid by a Canadian crown corporation. Alan Lawrence, who, since losing the provincial Conservative leadership contest in Ontario to Bill Davis, had been howling in the federal wilderness in Ottawa, seized upon the issue of "agent's fees" as a godsend to his career and devoted what remained of his political energies to making the issue a *cause célèbre*. "Agent's

J.L. Gray, president of Atomic Energy of Canada Limited, is seen here between Major General Georges Vanier and Madame Vanier during the visit of the governor general and his wife to the Chalk River Laboratories in October of 1966. This is an excellent portrait of Gray, who, some of us said, always looked like a character out of *The Godfather*. Gray is pointing out the features of the Douglas Point Generating Station, shown as a model in the foreground. Douglas Point itself was still under construction and commissioning in 1966. Beautifully executed models have always been a feature of the AECL program. This model was in the new and elegant Information Centre at Chalk River, characterized by Dr C.J. Mackenzie upon an earlier visit as "looking like a high-class cat-house." AECL Photo No. 6610-5533-59 fees" became a catchword in Ottawa for political sallies, puns, and general gossip, culminating in a thunderous denunciation of AECL in Parliament by the usually cheerful Don Mazankowski, caucus chairman for the opposition Progressive Conservatives. The situation was not put to rest until AECL paid formally for its alleged transgressions. John Foster, who had replaced Gray as president, was removed from office as a token of disciplinary action. Having done what damage he could, Lawrence faded from public life and was not heard from again. In point of fact, AECL made money on a successful Argentine project, and the Wolsung nuclear generating station became an outstanding success, to be repeated at a later date with a second CANDU station.

––––––––––

Lorne Gray, who had done so much to steer the fortunes of AECL through the mazes of Ottawa politics and who could claim credit for much of AECL's success, retired to Deep River and withdrew from professional life. He had been recognized by his old university with an LL.D. and granted a D.Sc. from the University of British Columbia. He had been awarded the Professional Engineers Gold Medal by the Association of Professional Engineers of the Province of Ontario in 1961. He had not been in good health upon retirement and lived quietly until his death in 1987 on his birthday, 2 March, at his home in Deep River. He was seventy-four years old. He had been predeceased for some years by his wife, Anne, who had remained frail after the difficult birth of their only child, Michael. The boy, too, had suffered, and was a source of worry throughout the lives of Lorne and Anne.

––––––––––

I have said that AECL's nuclear power program had its beginnings in the realization that practically all major sources of water power in Ontario had been developed, or would shortly be developed, and that any further expansion of electrical generating capacity would have to be from coal or from uranium. The argument against coal at the time was that it had to be imported from Pennsylvania and was a drain on our foreign exchange, whereas uranium was indigenous and in ample supply. With the passage of years, the arguments against coal have become far more persuasive. The emissions from any station burning coal, oil, or natural gas contribute mightily to the pollution of the atmosphere and to the accumulation of greenhouse gases, mainly carbon dioxide, whose effect is to raise gradually the surface temperature of the Earth, melting the polar ice caps and causing drastic flooding and climate change. Increasingly, international bodies have been warning of these effects. A report issued in February 2001 from Geneva by the Intergovernmental Panel on Climate Change paints a grim picture of the flooding of Florida, of a malaria zone stretching north to Britain, of deserts enveloping Nigeria, of freak storms ravaging Central America, and other catastrophes, if current practices are not modified for the better.

Coal-fired stations actually emit far more radioactivity (originating in the coal itself) and other pollutants than would be permitted from a nuclear station. METAALICUS, the international experiment coordinated by Trent University in Peterborough to determine the paths taken by mercury contamination that ends in fish in Canada and the United States, identifies the burning of coal, oil, and natural gas as the primary source of mercury in the atmosphere. Canada's ratification in 2003 of the international Kyoto Accord on greenhouse gas emissions is evidence of this country's recognition of the problems posed by fossil fuel.

There are, of course, alternatives to coal, oil, and natural gas. In certain applications wind power, biomass, and solar energy can be used, if they are found to be competitive with conventional fuels, or if, even when more expensive, there are compelling reasons for using them. It is fair to say, however, that these alternatives are generally so expensive as to be economically unattractive today and for the foreseeable future. More important is the fact that wind and solar power (and to some extent biomass) are low intensity energy sources that would require multiplication to astronomical numbers, even if this were practical, to supply a significant proportion of the energy needs of modern society. The current trend is to ever-larger concentrations of people in centres of population, requiring large sources of high intensity energy, a fact often ignored by the proponents of alternative energy strategies.

These proponents also argue that the very need for more energy can be avoided by implementing serious programs of conservation of the energy we have from existing sources. There is no question that conservation is an effective strategy. It is used in Switzerland, for example, where certain industries confine their operations to periods when the demand for electricity is low. But to be really effective in larger industrial societies conservation strategies demand massive societal changes, which are unlikely to be implemented in the foreseeable future.

If the world is to maintain, in the developed countries, and improve, in the developing countries, its standard of living without grievously impacting the environment, it is becoming more and more apparent that we must rely on energy from the atom. The Royal Society and the Royal Academy of Engineering in a 1999 British report and the Atlantic Council of the United States in a 2000 report have made this argument. Significantly, the Ontario government is, at the time of writing, broaching the need for further nuclear power in Ontario.

A nuclear station makes no contribution to the greenhouse effect. Uranium is abundant in Canada and it is possible in principle to put a nuclear-electric station wherever it is needed. However, nuclear-electric generation is no panacea. The fuel in a nuclear station becomes intensely radioactive, though the radioactivity is contained and manageable: the zirconium alloy sheath containing the fuel is extremely rugged and resistant to corrosion. In terms of human lifetimes the spent fuel must be safely stored "forever," and this aspect of using energy from the atom is a source of great concern. Those who maintain that nothing can be guaranteed "forever" have a valid point. However, the problems of permanent storage have been thoroughly examined over the last half-century both in Canada and elsewhere, and if safety cannot be guaranteed "forever," it can be as fully assured as human beings can make it. The most penetrating radiation disappears by natural decay in a relatively short time, and the longer-lived activity is mainly alpha and beta, which – as we have seen – are easily shielded against. There is also the fact that the quantity of nuclear waste is minuscule compared to the energy that has been produced, a fact colourfully illustrated by Philip Hammond of the Oak Ridge National Laboratory, who writes in the journal *AWARE*, "If New York City were entirely nuclear powered, the annual fission waste would approximate the volume of the mayor's limousine."

This is not strictly true, because the tiny volume of fission waste would be dispersed in a much larger volume of spent fuel and would not easily be separated from it, but the example has point. A great amount of energy is obtained from a very small amount of fuel.

In any event, we are unable to predict the future, so must do as best we can for the present. It is possible that future generations will find our arrangements inadequate. On the other hand, it is equally possible that they will find them more conservative than necessary.

Despite such drawbacks of nuclear-electric generation, it is likely to remain the option of choice in many circumstances and for many years to come. It is significant that the Japanese, the only people in the world to have suffered the horror of nuclear attack, chose to base their electrical industry on nuclear-electric generation. Their industrial success stems at least in part from a reliable and economical network of electrical power.

Their success has since been repeated in South Korea, where CANDU stations at Wolsung have been producing power for years. China, a major contributor to atmospheric pollution through its extensive network of coal-burning power stations, is seeking CANDU stations for future power generation. At the time of writing, the first Chinese CANDUs have started up. The European Directorate General of Energy concluded in 1999 that nuclear power is essential for Europe to meet its commitment to reduce greenhouse gas emissions. Cesare Marchetti of the International Agency for Applied Systems Analysis in Laxenburg, Austria, showed as early as 1980 that nuclear power applications, both for electricity generation and ship propulsion, promise to increase by market penetration well into the twenty-first century. It is the only current energy technology that is acceptable environmentally and capable of giving us a realistic energy bridge into the future

It is true that the operation of nuclear power stations calls for very special knowledge and techniques not usually found in other industries. This has in the past been a point of attack by the anti-nuclear establishment. Our dependence on the electrical power from nuclear stations has been decried by critics as our being at the mercy of a "nuclear priesthood." If such a charge ever had weight, it lacks impact in today's high-tech society. Nuclear power specialists may be likened to a "priesthood" of sorts, but no more so than, say, the medical fraternity, computer specialists, or any other highly specialized group.

It is often difficult for those in the nuclear industry to appreciate the problems raised by technical ignorance among the general population, but it is important to recognize that the ignorance exists and to factor it into any plans for nuclear power. It is generally an ignorance that has little interest in, or patience with, specific technical details, but it is sharply focused on individual advantage and well-being, as indeed might be expected. I recall that Dr O.J.C. Runnalls, one of the best public speakers at the Chalk River Project, took part in one of the speakers' bureaus that the Project operated in the fifties and sixties for the benefit of the surrounding communities. After one of his better efforts in describing the aims and objectives of the Chalk River program and what it held for the future of the country, he asked for questions. The first person to raise a hand asked, "How much do you make?"

There is, in some circles, a serious distrust of the nuclear industry in Canada. The source of this is difficult to pinpoint, though it is fair to say that almost any human endeavour, if it is large enough and pervasive enough, will attract groups of protestors, and nuclear power is surely a special case. As happens so often, anti-nuclear attitudes in Canada may have developed from attitudes in the United States. As I have noted, distrust may have grown there as a reaction to the high-handed operations of the U.S. Atomic Energy Commission, which inherited from the wartime operations of the Manhattan Project a stance almost of "divine right" in many of its approaches to matters of public interest. There arose a culture among some well-educated Americans that was devoted to challenging the accepted wisdom of the USAEC and that produced articulate critics adept at seizing the limelight. American representatives of this culture were often invited to address meetings in Canada. It may also have been that attack on institutions and established authority was a common North American phenomenon in the sixties and seventies. Claude Bissell, president of the University of Toronto, in writing about his clash with U of T undergraduates of that era, speaks of the "icy contempt of youth." Some of the main Canadian figures in the domestic anti-nuclear movements were educated in the States during the tumultuous sixties, and some of them are still active today.

Their commitment to opposing nuclear power, taken together with the lack of knowledge of the general population, make for volatile situations when major nuclear decisions are to be taken.

Critics in the United States maintained that the American program of nuclear-electric generation was formulated in an atmosphere of blind enthusiasm for atomic energy without due consideration for the real costs involved. This was brought out clearly in a 1981 work by Peter Pringle and James Spigelman entitled *The Nuclear Barons*, hailed at the time by the *Washington Post* as "An exceptional book...[that reveals] the human foibles and well-intentioned blunders at the heart of the nuclear mess." As an example, U.S. General Electric's problems with "turn-key" contracts (mentioned here in chapter 6) were attributed to ambitious proposals made without reference to the eventual costs of nuclear plants. In fact, the cost problem stemmed from the fact that the early American plants operated at their designed capacities only 50 to 60 per cent of the time. More recently, improved techniques of operation have increased these percentages to 90 per cent and above, almost doubling the power available from existing installations.

Canada's choice of heavy water/natural uranium reactors made it necessary to monitor costs carefully with every step of development. A "fever chart" of the cost of electricity (mills/kilowatt hour) was the control against which every design decision was made. In other respects, also, the situation in Canada was different from that in the United States. Ontario Hydro and AECL could hardly be said to be in competition as were General Electric and Westinghouse, and there was no incentive to cut corners and underestimate costs.

Similarly, opposition to nuclear power differed in the two countries. Whereas in the United States the anti-nuclear movement often became confrontational, with the toppling of meteorological towers, tearing down of fences, and the like, in Canada the movement inspired a more soul-searching approach. In Ontario in the seventies and early eighties innumerable meetings were held at which the pros and cons of nuclear power development were aired. These were not debates so much as statements of irreconcilably opposing views, and they produced few, if any, compromises. The (now defunct) Science Council of Canada organized a conference with the title "A Nuclear Dialogue," held at the Guild Inn in Toronto in March 1976, to which the major anti-nuclear figures in Canada and the United States were invited to exchange ideas with proponents of nuclear development. The conference did little beside raise the temperature of argument. Andy Potworowski of the Science Council, in reporting on the "Dialogue," wrote, "almost everyone seemed to agree that better public information was desirable, [but] it was apparent that, under the surface, this was for two different reasons. Some participants believed that if the public were well informed they would solidly support nuclear; others believed that if the public could get the truth about nuclear they would solidly oppose it."

In Deep River, Reverend Allen Box, the local Anglican priest, organized with help from an enthusiastic committee a conference entitled "Shaping the Future" over a long weekend in October 1976. The conference had the support of the Canada Council, the Anglican, Roman Catholic, and Lutheran churches, the Royal Commission on Electric Power Planning, and the town of Deep River. The conference drew distinguished participants from all over Canada, though most of those attending were from Deep River itself. "Shaping the Future" was a brave attempt to identify and discuss issues raised by the intersection of theology with science and technology, particularly nuclear science and technology. A keynote speaker was Dr W.G. Pollard, a nuclear physicist and priest-in-charge at Christ Church, Rugby, Tennessee, who spoke on "Energy and the Conquest of Fear." He concluded that "to refuse the blessing for fear of the curse is no reasonable course to take." One must "maximize the blessing and minimize the curse." The Sister Superior of Madonna House in Combermere, Ontario, then rose and, in an impassioned address, offered the audience the choice between "The Baby and the Bomb." After it was all over, Allen Box in his summary report had to admit, somewhat ruefully, that those who came with an anti-nuclear bias went away with the same bias, and that proponents of nuclear power remained just as positive after the conference. It was almost as though the conference was dealing with two fundamentally different aspects of the human psyche, one positive in regard to nuclear energy and one negative. There was apparently no common ground between the two camps and it was pointless for them to discuss and argue about something on which they could never agree.

———.

1976 was a peak year for this sort of dialogue, if dialogue it can be called, though the controversy continued into the eighties and nineties and is with us to the present day. In 1976 the World Council of Churches, in an attempt to arrive at a balanced view of the situation, issued a summary statement to the effect that "nuclear energy epitomizes the dilemma of infinite potential benefit coupled with infinite risk to the community at large." I wonder to what extent that statement was supported by the scientists and engineers of the World Council. One supposes that "infinite risk" describes a common perception of the potential hazard of operating a nuclear power station. The terrible accident at Chernobyl has probably done much to reinforce such a perception, though in reality Chernobyl did not pose infinite risks even in consequence of almost criminal mismanagement by the Russians, and the undamaged reactor is back in operation. It is the task of scientists and engineers to extract useful energy from the atom while minimizing risk to an acceptable level. The "dilemma" suffered by the World Council of Churches must have existed for those who could not accept any level of risk, however minimal.

Anglican Archbishop Ted Scott, a member of the World Council of Churches who attended the conference of 1976 in Deep River, was invited to speak at the annual meeting of the Canadian Nuclear Association later that year. He caused a flurry by pronouncing nuclear power not worth the risks it entailed. The reaction was immediate and acrimonious. Lorne Gray, the AECL past president, showed a degree of anger seldom seen in public. In a reply to Scott, Dr Omond Solandt, in introducing his own paper, "The Predicaments of Man," said that, while he did not doubt the sincerity of the archbishop's convictions, he would question his competence to make such a statement. The Primate's negative verdict must indeed have been disappointing for Christians who considered the discovery of atomic energy as merely the most recent revelation of the awe and wonder of God's universe. Surely, the intelligent use of this source of energy for human benefit is nothing more than the application of the principle illustrated in the "Parable of the Talents."

For some, the use of atomic power appears inextricably linked with the atomic bomb, the sinister side of nuclear energy, and this must surely influence attitudes of these individuals in a deeply personal way. One wonders whether such attitudes may have influenced the deliberations of the World Council of Churches. If atomic energy has a dark side, it only reflects the dark side of humanity itself, the will to inflict hurt on other humans. As in other instances, God has left it to human free will to make the choice for good or evil in the use of this source of energy.

————

The anti-nuclear critics will always be there and it is an important aspect of their agenda to persuade the public of impending disaster. To counter this, the nuclear industry must always be as open as possible with the public, even at the risk of frightening the more timid. An example can be found in the unique rupture of a single pressure tube (among the hundreds of such tubes in Canadian reactors) that occurred in 1981 in a reactor of the Pickering "A" nuclear generating station. The accident was handled very professionally by the staff of the station and the community of Pickering was never at risk, but the incident was given minimum coverage in the media. Yet it was a blazing example of the soundness of the CANDU design and the competence of a well-trained operating staff. All of this could have been brought out in public by televised replays of techniques, interviews with staff, animated diagrams, and explanatory talks.

Canadian opposition to atomic energy may be vastly overestimated, though periodic Decima polls made for AECL appear to indicate a fairly steady opposition among 15 to 20 per cent of those polled. The predilection of the popular press for seizing upon any conflict of opinion for elaboration and amplification makes it possible for a small, well organized vocal minority to appear much larger than it is. If, however, opposition is in fact widespread among Canadians, it would appear not only reasonable but necessary for the federal government, which supports AECL and the Canadian Nuclear Safety Commission (the former Atomic Energy Control Board) to provide support for a third organization of the critics and opponents of nuclear power. Such support would legitimize the opposition, would make it incumbent upon the nay-sayers to meet the professional standards demanded of AECL and CNSC, and would be conditional upon meeting such standards. The process would have the advantage of bringing the opposition out into the open and evaluating it. It would have the added advantage that publicity would be in the form of reports and press releases from an established organization rather than from whimsical interviews with individuals. Such a course of action would appear to be a considerable improvement over current discourse. Whether it would succeed in satisfying the demands of nuclear critics is open to question, but it might identify criticism from cranks and idiosyncratics as being outside the realm of rational discussion. It might also deprive the popular press of an important source of conflict and confrontation.

A proposal for government sponsorship of an organization for nuclear critics raises the interesting question of what such an organization should be called. Most of the existing organizations supporting nuclear critics and dissidents have chosen names that adopt the moral high ground and by implication condemn opposition to them as being inimical, irresponsible, or simply misguided. Thus, "Friends of the Earth" by the very name implies that anyone in opposition is no friend of the Earth, and organizations, let us say, for "Nuclear Responsibility" beg the question whether anyone outside of the organization can be considered socially "responsible." In order to be fair, the name must not be loaded in this way, and it will be a nice problem to choose a name that does not imply reproach of those producing or using nuclear power.

Those employed in the nuclear industry demand, consciously or unconsciously, enormous trust on the part of those whom they serve. Trust is a priceless commodity. It must be earned and once earned must be guarded and maintained with every means at one's disposal. The education and training of scientists and engineers does not devote much effort to this aspect of professional life, if it deals with it at all. We have much to learn from the medical profession in this regard (though even here there appear to be breaches of trust). How often have we witnessed the sorry spectacle of a scientist or an engineer trying to respond in intelligible terms to questions raised by a concerned public? Yet polls have shown time and again that, in spite of this deficiency, scientists and engineers rank high in public esteem, just as lawyers and politicians, perhaps undeservedly, rank at the bottom of the list. The potential for trust is there. The trust must be earned. In view of the potential risks perceived by the community at large, this is more important to the nuclear industry than to any other. And this applies to Canada as much as to any country in the world.

———.

The trust of the common Canadian was not, unfortunately, often encouraged and nourished by the pronouncements of W.B. Lewis. He had the honest conviction that atomic energy would be used for the eventual benefit of humankind, but was so little a participant in the common world around him that he was relatively insensitive to public concerns and was at a loss to communicate his vision to Canadians generally. This was no fault of his. He had come from Britain to Canada at the age of thirty-eight, bringing with him high honours in recognition of his wartime services. He had no particular wish to put his past behind him, and, living as he did with his mother, he was to some extent anchored in his past. He did his best to enter into the life of Deep River, but his senior position, together with his personal tastes and eccentricities, tended to exclude him from informal and intimate society. His speaking manner was diffident and hesitating and to the uninitiated he appeared unsure of his convictions. Nothing, of course, could be further from the truth. However, he would have been crucified publicly by today's thirty-second sound-bites.

If his public persona could be something of a liability, his professional contributions to science and engineering more than made up for this defect. His work was widely recognized both nationally and internationally. He deserved, as no one else did, the title of "Father of the CANDU Reactor." He received the first ever Outstanding Achievement Award of the Public Service of Canada. He shared the international Atoms For Peace Award for his contributions, through the United Nations

Geneva Conferences, to the peaceful uses of atomic energy. The Canadian Association of Physicists struck a special gold medal, the W.B. Lewis Medal, in recognition of his support of fundamental science at Chalk River. The premier award of the Canadian Nuclear Association was named after him. He received at different times honorary doctorates in science and laws from ten Canadian universities. He was the first Canadian citizen to receive the Enrico Fermi Award from the United States Department of Energy. As an Honorary Fellow of the Institute of Electrical Engineers he is listed with such names as Edison, Marconi, and Alexander Graham Bell.

——————

Lewis retired "full of honours" from AECL in 1973. A retirement party was held at Deep River to which came friends, associates, and colleagues from Canada and the United States. I drove up to Deep River from Lakefield for the occasion. When my turn came, I thanked W.B. for "making my life so interesting and exciting." Gwynned Gary, his sister, who was standing beside him, reacted emotionally to this, but W.B. seemed at a loss for a reply.

For some years Lewis continued to lecture and write as a Distinguished Professor of Science at Queen's University until he was overtaken by declining health. Tragically, he suffered a collapse of his mental powers in his last years and was cared for by Gwynned, who had taken over the household upon the death of their mother. He died in Deep River in his seventy-ninth year on 10 January 1987. For scientists and engineers in Canada his death marked the end of an era, an era that saw, as Lorne Gray said, the expansion of Canada's efforts in the field of atomic energy from a cluster of laboratories on the shore of the Ottawa River to the development of a major industry stretching from coast to coast and overseas. CANDU's production of electricity from the energy within the atom has become commonplace.

W.B. Lewis at the head of the pack. The cover of the April 1977 issue of *Nuclear Engineering International* shows Lewis front and centre and the only figure actively doing something. He has his hand on the shoulder of Sigvard Eklund, director general of the International Atomic Energy Agency. To Eklund's left is Prof. Arnaldo M. Angelini, president of the Italian national electricity authority and a fan of the CANDU nuclear power system. Just behind him is Prof. Jules Guéron, who played such an important role in the Montreal Laboratory during World War II. The caricatures are all very good. Courtesy of *Nuclear Engineering International*, London

Starting in the upper left (three rows of four), Chet Holifield, John W. Simpson, Edward Teller, the Lord Hinton o' Bankside; Jules Guéron, Prof. Schulten, Norman Rasmussen, Ted Shaw; Prof. Arnaldo M. Angelini, Sigvard Eklund, W.B. Lewis, Prof. Dr Heinrich Mandel

————.

The Ottawa River has always had an important and colourful role in Canada's growth and development. Carved along the edge of the Laurentian range by the waters of the melting ice cap during the last age of glaciers, it has been the chief drainage system of an enormous area of the interior for at least ten thousand years. In time, it became a major travel route for early humans. Thousands of years later it led explorers and adventurers into the interior. In the seventeenth and eighteenth centuries it brought furs to markets in the east. The old trading post at Fort William still has the pattern for a freight canoe in one of its sheds. In the nineteenth and early twentieth centuries the river floated out of the interior great rafts of white pine for British naval masts and squared timbers for European markets. From 1945 onward it was intimately involved with the operation of ZEEP, NRX, NRU, and NPD, and so the story of Canada's adventure into the nuclear age forms the most recent pattern in the rich tapestry of the river's history. It is a pattern that traces in detail the early development of the CANDU nuclear-electric generating station, Canada's contribution to the peaceful uses of atomic energy and an outstanding achievement of science and engineering of the twentieth century.

————.

At their appointed times and in their separate ways, both Lewis and Gray died beside the Ottawa River. Each had devoted a full complement of extraordinary talents and energy into bringing Canada's nuclear program from its modest beginnings to a national industry. Their achievement is now part of the river's story.

References

The reader will appreciate that much of what I have written in *Deep Waters* comes from personal experience and recollection. He or she may be interested in pursuing the story further or in seeking some corroboration, and to that end I have appended these references. Most of the material is from files and publications in my own library. I have included a brief commentary on each of the publications as a guide to the reader unfamiliar with the field. Information on the historical background of Deep River and the region comes from Joan Melvin (18), Mrs Carl Price and Clyde Kennedy (20), and Charlotte Whitton (26). For historical information on Canada's program of nuclear power development I have on occasion consulted Eggleston (4), Bothwell (3), Margaret Gowing (6), and W.B. Lewis (13), as well as the annual reports of Atomic Energy of Canada Limited (1). For verification of technical information the compendium edited by Don Hurst (9) has been invaluable not only for details of the Canadian program but for general references as well. Information on critics of nuclear power comes from the work of Amory Lovins (15, 16), Walter Patterson (19), and Pringle and Spigelman (21). Archie Robertson (22) provides a useful discussion of pro- and anti-nuclear arguments. These and other useful references, not referred to by number above, are listed alphabetically below.

1   Atomic Energy of Canada Limited, *Annual Reports*. Beginning in
    1952–53, these reports are a goldmine of information on the develop-
    ment of nuclear science and nuclear power in Canada, though they
    are made more interesting if one knows the stories behind the reports.
    A case in point is the report for 1976-77, celebrating "Twenty-five Years
    of Nuclear Progress," which features a long and eloquent letter of
    transmittal from Ross Campbell, chairman of the board, to his minis-
    ter, Alastair Gillespie, responding to the furor in Ottawa over the pro-
    jected losses of the Argentine contract and the hiring of an agent for
    the sale to South Korea. The situation is described in the epilogue of
    Deep Waters.

2   Bhabha, Homi J. *Nuclear Disarmament,* text of a broadcast over All India
    Radio, 24 October 1964. Reported in *Nuclear India* 3, no.3, November
    1964. Homi Bhabha was one of several Indian graduate students
    studying at Cambridge in the 1930s. He was a friend and colleague of
    J.D. Cockcroft and W.B. Lewis, and after World War II he became
    director general of the Indian Department of Atomic Energy. The
    broadcast was given after the first explosion of a nuclear device by
    China. He points out that "neither the United Nations nor the great
    powers have yet succeeded in creating a climate favourable to coun-
    tries which have the capability of making atomic weapons, but have
    voluntarily refrained from doing so. Steps must be taken to create
    such a climate as early as possible." Dr Bhabha's reasonable voice was
    cut off by an untimely death in a plane crash in 1966. In his absence,
    the "bomb faction" in the Department of Atomic Energy flourished
    and India detonated a "peaceful" atomic explosion in 1974.

3   Bothwell, Robert. *NUCLEUS: The History of Atomic Energy of Canada Limited*,
    University of Toronto Press, 1988. Prof. Bothwell is a Trinity College
    historian who, when invited to write this history, protested that he did
    not have the technical background to deal with the subject. He has
    nevertheless produced a remarkable work – on the scale of Margaret
    Gowing's history – that traces in detail the history of AECL from a non-
    technical point of view up to within a few months of the date of publi-
    cation. There are extensive notes and an index.

4   Eggleston, Wilfrid. *Canada's Nuclear Story*, Clarke, Irwin, Toronto, 1965.
    Although I was disparaging of this work when asked to review chap-
    ters during its production, I have since found it a useful reference. It
    has a foreword by Dr C.J. Mackenzie.

5   Goldschmidt, Bertrand. *The Atomic Adventure: Its Political Aspects*, Pergamon
    Press, London, 1964. The atomic story told from the French point of
    view by a scientist who knew many of the chief proponents of *The*

Atomic Adventure personally, if not intimately. Goldschmidt was a radio-chemist and member of the international team at the Montreal Laboratory. His version of the theft of samples from the laboratory by Alan Nunn May is unique in that he says it was uranium-233, not plu-tonium, that was taken.

6   Gowing, Margaret. *Britain and Atomic Energy 1939-1945*, Macmillan, London, 1964. Margaret Gowing was the historian and archivist for the United Kingdom Atomic Energy Authority. This is a superb history of wartime developments in atomic energy from the British point of view.

7   Hahn, Otto. *My Life*, translated from *Mein Leben*, 1968, by Kaiser and Wilkins, Herder and Herder, New York, 1970. As chemists, Hahn and Strassmann missed the significance of the fissioning of uranium by slow neutrons because they worked with the *atomic weights* of the products, whereas the *atomic numbers* indicated clearly what had happened. Hahn draws his description of the effect of his transmission to Lise Meitner of the paper describing this work from Laura Fermi's account in her book, *The Story of Atomic Energy*.

8   Heisenberg, Werner. *Der Teil und Das Ganze,* Piper & Co. Verlag, Munich, 1969. Heisenberg's autobiography gives an interesting account, written at some distance in time from the events described, and under vastly altered circumstances, of his and Weizacker's reactions to the possible development of an atomic weapon. They were horrified by the thought, but had to wonder if they would proceed with the task if required by their government. They had also to consider what former colleagues who were now refugees in the U.S. would choose to do under similar circumstances.

9   Hurst, D.G., and E. Critoph, A.M. Marko, D.K. Myers, F.C. Boyd, B. Ullyet, G.C. Hanna, T.A. Eastwood, J.C.D. Milton, H.K. Rae, M.F. Duret, C.E. Ells, A.S. Bain, R.E. Green, R.G. Hart, J.A.L. Robertson, *Canada Enters the Nuclear Age: A Technical History of Atomic Energy of Canada Limited*, McGill-Queen's University Press, Montreal, 1997. Don Hurst is a physicist who has been with the Canadian project since the days of the Montreal Laboratory. He was intimately involved in every major development at the Chalk River Laboratories of AECL, and, next to W.B. Lewis, is the most qualified person to write such a technical history. The other authors are, with few exceptions, AECL scientists, each a major figure in his field. This provides a technical history of the development of the CANDU nuclear power reactor, AECL's major technical achievement, and supplements Bothwell's work referred to above. The unique qualities and characteristics of the Canadian program, which

allowed Canada to bring the CANDU concept to fruition at a fraction of the cost expended in the development programs of other countries, are clearly described and explained in a final chapter by J.A.L. Robertson. This chapter alone deserves publication on its own. The book is in coffee table format, but while it is an invaluable reference book for someone like myself, it is heavy going for even the most passionately devoted general reader. Each chapter has extensive notes, and the book has an index.

10   Lapp, Ralph E. *Radioactive Waste: Society's Problem Child*, Reddy Communications Inc., Greenwich, Conn., 1977. Ralph Lapp is a physicist with impeccable qualifications who was one of the early opponents of atmospheric testing of nuclear weapons. He then became an independent consultant. This little book is a very effective presentation for the general reader of the realities of nuclear waste disposal, a "child" whose "problems" are largely misunderstood by the public and misrepresented by the media.

11   Laurence, George C. *Early Years of Nuclear Research in Canada*, Atomic Energy of Canada Limited, Chalk River Nuclear Laboratories, 1980. As explained in the text of *Deep Waters*, George Laurence deserves more than any other Canadian to be remembered as a pioneer in atomic energy. This slim publication gives an accurate technical history of the work done in the Montreal Laboratory leading up to the completion of the ZEEP reactor at Chalk River. Laurence made significant contributions to reactor design with NRU, nuclear safeguards at the International Atomic Energy Agency, and reactor safety with the Atomic Energy Control Board.

12   Lewis, W.B. *The Accident to the NRX Reactor on December 12, 1952*, Atomic Energy of Canada Report AECL-232, 1953. This is an authoritative report on the NRX accident that is described briefly in *Deep Waters*. My version was arrived at in consultation with Dr L.G. McConnell, who took charge of the situation in the NRX building within minutes of the accident.

13   Lewis, W.B. *Canada's Steps toward Nuclear Power,* Atomic Energy of Canada Report AECL-593, 1958. This paper, prepared for the Second International Conference on the Peaceful Uses of Atomic Energy, is the earliest comprehensive review of the steps by which Canada proposed to achieve electrical generation from atomic power at costs competitive with power from conventional sources. The history of CANDU development is in a very real sense the history of work done at Chalk River to implement the ideas described in AECL-593.

14   Lewis, W.B., and A.G. Ward. *An Appreciation of the Problem of Reactor Shut-off Rods With Special Reference to the NRX Reactor*, Atomic Energy of Canada Report DR-31, 1953. A critical review of the problems presented by the NRX shut-off mechanisms that contributed to the NRX accident.

15   Lovins, Amory B. "Energy Strategy: The Road Not Taken," *Foreign Affairs*, October 1976. This article appeared at the height of Lovins' influence on public opinion, particularly among those opposed to nuclear power. It is an elaboration on *Non-Nuclear Futures*, noted below. Lovins is a vigorous promoter of alternative energy strategies such as conservation, wind, and solar. J.A.L. Robertson calls him a "dangerous man," for he is selling an idyllic future without showing the price tag.

16   Lovins, Amory B., and John H. Price. *Non-Nuclear Futures: The Case for an Ethical Energy Strategy,* Friends of the Earth, Ballinger, New York, 1975. Lovins is a brilliant, articulate, and persuasive critic of nuclear power as a present and future source of energy. An American, he resigned a Junior Research Fellowship at Merton College, Oxford, to become British representative of Friends of the Earth, an American non-profit conservation group. Ethical questions arise from the necessity of burdening future generations with the long-lived radioactive waste from nuclear stations. Lovins and Price also raise the question of the net energy gain from operating a nuclear station; that is, is the output from such a station significantly greater than the sum of all the energy going into building and fueling the station? Their figures indicate that it is not. However, the experience of the past thirty years would indicate that they have been unnecessarily pessimistic.

17   Marchetti, Cesare. *Nuclear Plants and Nuclear Niches*, International Institute for Applied Systems Analysis, A-2361 Laxenburg, Austria, 1985. Marchetti was my branch head at the Euratom laboratory in Ispra, Italy. He left Euratom shortly after I returned to Canada and joined the Laxenburg Institute, where he specialized in the study of the market penetration of different energy technologies. This is only one of a series of reports applying the measurement of market penetration over long periods of time of a variety of energy technologies.

18   Melvin, Joan. *Deep River, 1945-1995: A Pictorial History*, jomel publications, Deep River, 1995. This is a splendid compilation of photographs of people, events, and venues associated with the village of Deep River from its start in 1945 to its fiftieth anniversary on the date of publication. Joan Melvin has provided a descriptive text that is the fruit of extensive and rigorous research.

19   Patterson, Walter C. *Nuclear Power*, Penguin Books, London, 1976.
     A readable account with a useful survey of early reactor types (which,
     incidentally, rates the safety of CANDU highly). Patterson is that rare
     creature, a physicist who writes with facility in terms that are easily
     grasped by the general reader. As a staff member of Friends of the
     Earth, his position on nuclear power is largely negative, but the treat-
     ment of his material is even-handed. There is an index.

20   Price, Mrs Carl, and Clyde C. Kennedy. *Notes on the History of Renfrew
     County,* Renfrew County Council, Pembroke, 1961. Clyde Kennedy was
     a senior AECL public relations officer based at the Chalk River Nuclear
     Laboratories. He had a deep interest in the history and archeology
     of the region and published much original work in archeological jour-
     nals. Mrs Price was a historian with the Ottawa Valley Historical
     Society. This book was produced for the centennial year, 1961. It is a
     kaleidoscope of Valley history, both ancient and modern.

21   Pringle, Peter, and James Spigelman. *The Nuclear Barons*, Avon Books,
     New York, 1981. Pringle is a British journalist and Spigelman an
     Australian who has held senior advisory positions in the Australian
     government. They have produced a highly readable account of the
     development of atomic energy, first in the sphere of nuclear weapons
     and later in the sphere of nuclear-electric generating stations. The
     "barons" are portrayed as an elite club of scientists, politicians, tech-
     nocrats, and big businessmen who have "pushed our civilization to
     the brink of annihilation." As will be imagined, much of the book has
     been written in an accusing tone. However, it is well documented and
     there is an extensive bibliography and an index.

22   Robertson, J.A.L. *Final Argument Relating to the Canadian Nuclear Power
     Program,* A Brief to the Ontario Royal Commission on Electric Power
     Planning. Atomic Energy of Canada Report AECL-6200, 1978. Archie
     Robertson is well known in the atomic energy community as a distin-
     guished scientist and as a writer and public speaker of great rigour
     and clarity. In this brief he defines the positions of several of the anti-
     nuclear activists of the day in terms of what they have put before the
     commission and compares these with the positions of established
     organizations in the field.

23   Robertson, J.A.L. *Nuclear Need Not Be Unclear: Decide the Nuclear Issues for
     Yourself,* Internet: http://www.magma.ca/~jalrober, 2000. This work
     was published on the Internet when Robertson could not find a firm
     that would publish it in book form. It has since attracted wide interest

on the Internet as a commentary in plain language on a subject that has all too often suffered at the hands of journalists and others lacking the qualifications, experience, and expertise of the author. It deserves attention today as never before, owing to the regained importance of nuclear power.

24 Siddall, E. *Reactor Safety Standards and Their Attainment*, Atomic Energy of Canada Report CRNE-726, 1957. Ernie Siddall's report represents an early attempt to answer the question "How safe is safe enough?" That is, at what point does increasing safety lead to diminished returns? The approach is unique and original and of sufficient importance to have elicited a foreword by W.B. Lewis. The basic problem is a "failure to understand that the intrinsic danger of a process has little or no relationship to the effective danger which it actually presents." As an example, the annual production of insecticides (mainly for food production) in the U.S. exceeds 15 *billion* doses fatal to human beings. Yet death from insecticides is rare. Such considerations apply to the pronouncements of the World Council of Churches on power from the atom quoted in the epilogue.

25 Weinberg, Alvin M. "Salvaging the Atomic Age," *The Wilson Quarterly*, Summer 1979. Weinberg was a major figure in atomic energy in the United States and a long-time director of the Oak Ridge National Laboratory. This long article is a sober reflection on the implications of the U.S. Atomic Energy Act of 1954, which took atomic energy out of the hands of government and turned it over to private industry. As can be gathered from the title, Weinberg was already perceiving a general disenchantment with atomic energy in the U.S. in 1979. His recommendation for the future was to restrict the building of new nuclear-electric generating stations to a series of sites remote from the general public and which would be devoted exclusively to nuclear power generation. This is precisely what has been achieved with the Canadian installations on Lake Huron.

26 Whitton, Charlotte. *A Hundred Years A'Fellin'*, originally printed for Gillies Brothers Limited, Braeside, Ontario, 1943. Reprinted by Runge Press, Ottawa, 1974. Charlotte Whitton had a brilliant academic career at Queen's University during WW I, went on to social work and municipal politics, and became mayor of Ottawa in 1951 – Canada's first woman mayor. A native of the Ottawa Valley, she had a reputation as a scholarly historian steeped in the Valley's history. She was commissioned by David Gillies to write the history of his company and its relation to the history of the Valley. The work is a treasure trove of history.

Index

Adams, Henry, 38
Alcock, Norman Z., 86
alpha, beta, and gamma radiation, 46, 49
Andognini, Carl, 130, 131
anti-nuclear activists, 104, 105
Argonne National Laboratory, 77
Atlantic Council of the U.S., 143
atomic energy, 89
Atomic Energy Control Board (now the Canadian Nuclear Safety Commission), 123
Atomic Energy of Canada Limited (AECL), 8, 94; partnership with Ontario Hydro, 132
atomic explosions at Hiroshima and Nagasaki, 26, 61, 66
Atoms for Peace Conference, 73

Bechtel Corporation, 135
Bennett, W.J., 127, 128
Bissell, Claude, 146
Bhabha, Homi, 138
Bhutto, President Zulfikar Ali, 134
Bland, John, 26
Bohr, Niels, 63, 65
Boom Man, 40
Box, Rev. Allen, 148, 149

Boyd, Winnett, 102, 103, 115
Brockhouse, Bertram, 86
Brooks, David, 9
Brunton, Donald, 85, 86
Buck, Tim, 71, 72
Burge, Ray, 74

Cameron, Alistair G.W., 86
Canadian General Electric Co., 9, 112, 113, 122, 123; Civilian Atomic Power Dept., 9, 113, 122; export program transferred to AECL, 139
Canadian Nuclear Safety Commission, 151
CANDU, 8, 11, 12, 127, 130, 134; "reactor of a thousand leaks," 100
Carmichael, Hugh, 58
Cavendish Laboratory, 6, 79
Chalk River, 17-19
Chalk River Project, 22
Chalk River Nuclear Laboratories (now Chalk River Laboratories), 122; contracting expertise, 132
Chadwick, (Sir) James, 64
Chernobyl, 73, 149
Churchill, Gordon, 129
Cockcroft, (Sir) John D., 26, 27, 30, 33, 69, 70, 78

Cohen, Paul, 99
Commission pour l'Energie
    Atomique, 54
Commonwealth Air Training
    Plan, 36
Community Centre, Deep River, 36
Cook, Leslie G., 80
Côté, Lucien, 25, 43, 68
CRUD (Chalk River Unidentified
    Deposit), 54
Cruikshank, Alec, 111
Curie, Mme. Marie Sklodowska,
    31, 32, 46, 49

Dainton, Prof. Fred S., 24
Davies, John A., 86
Davis, Bill, 139
Deep River, 7, 8, 13, 18, 26, 124;
    Aboriginal families, 14, 18, 87;
    concentration of Ph.D.s, 54,
    58, 134
Defence Industries Limited (DIL),
    5, 21
Desbarats, H.J., 22, 35
Douglas Point, 129, 130

Edwards, Prof. Gordon, 108
Energy, Mines and Resources,
    Dept of, 9; Energy Conservation
    Branch, 9
European Directorate General of
    Energy, 145
Export Credit Insurance
    Corporation, 123

Ferguson, John, 56
Finniston, Monty, 22
fission, 63, 77
Foster, John, 10, 125, 136, 137
Franck, James, 65
Fraser Brace Construction, 21,
    24, 78
Fraser's Landing, 3, 92
Freundlich, Herbert F., 81

Frisch, Otto, 63
Frost, Leslie M., 114

Gary, Gwynned, 154
General Electric Co., 9
Gilbert, C.W., 77
Gillies Brothers of Arnprior, 16, 41;
    Gillies, David, 16, 44
Goldschmidt, Bertrand, 31, 32
Gouzenko, Igor, 70
Gray, J. Lorne, 9, 83, 115, 127-9,
    137-9, 141
Groves, Gen. Leslie R., 61
Grummitt, W.E., 59, 105, 106
Guéron, Jules, 70, 155
Guggenheim, Prof. E.A., 29

Hahn, Otto, 62, 63
Halban, Hans von, 30, 69
Harris, Mike, 131
Harvey, Bernard G., 94, 95
Harwell, 27, 78
Hatfield, Gordie, 5, 7, 68
Health Radiation Branch, 32, 50, 84
heavy water, 52, 88
Heisenberg, Werner, 26
Howe, Clarence Decatur, 102,
    114, 127
Hurst, Don G., 92
Hydro One Networks, 132

Imperial Chemical Industries, 5
Indian families at Deep River, 16
Indian NRX reactor, 138
Industry, Trade and Commerce,
    Dept of, 123
Institut de Radium, Paris, 32
isotopes, 88-90

Joliot, Frédéric, 52, 64, 69

KANUPP, 124
King, W.L. Mackenzie, 70
Kinsey, Bernard B., 34

Kirkwood, Dave H.W., 81
Kowarski, Lew, 30, 35, 52-4, 88; and
    H. von Halban, 64; name missing
    from ZEEP plaque, 82

Laurence, George C., 6, 79, 83;
    design of NRU, 102
Lawrence, Alan, 139
Lawrence, N. Quentin, 24
Lewis, David, 97, 100
Lewis, Isoline, 83, 111, 112
Lewis, W.B., 79-81, 83, 85, 86, 92,
    94, 138, 153, 154; CANDU, 127,
    138, 153, 154; clash with Rickover,
    100; development of NRU, 101;
    and Y-flyer, 11, 112
Lily St Cyr, 51
Little, Eileen, 31
Lustman, Ben, 97

Maddock, A.G., 70
Manhattan Project, 66, 70, 71,
    88, 146
Marchetti, Cesare, 108, 145
Martin, Charles, 41
May, Alan Nunn, 70, 71
Mazankowski, Don, 141
McConnachie, Peter, 68
McConnell, Lorne G., 24, 121
McElligott, Father, 16, 36, 45, 56
MacKay, Ian, 25, 43
Mackenzie, C.J., 94, 95, 102, 127;
    president of AECL, 94
MDS-Nordion, 90
Meitner, Lise, 62, 65
Mercereau, Adeline, 45
METAALICUS international
    program, 142
Miller, Charlie, 57
Miller, Nicholas, 7
Montreal Laboratory, 5, 6, 21,
    31, 71
Montreal University, 51, 67, 77
Moodie, Norm, 80, 81

National Research Council of
    Canada (NRC), 6, 10, 21, 22, 79
Nautilus nuclear submarine, 96, 100
neutrons, 64
Newcombe, Howard, 108
NPD (Nuclear Power
    Demonstration), 112-15, 118, 119,
    120, 121; fuel development, 116,
    117; fueling machines, 120, 121
NRU (National Research Universal),
    101-4
NRX (National Research
    Experiment), 52, 68, 76, 77, 83;
    1952 accident, 84, 93-5; loops
    in the reactor, 98; production of
    isotopes, 90, 93; start-up, 92;
    submarine program (U.S.), 96
nuclear energy, 89
Nuclear Power Plant Division, 125

Ontario Hydro, 108, 109, 113, 122,
    127, 131
Ontario Power Generation, 131
Ottawa River, 11, 13, 38, 39, 76,
    91, 156

Pakistan, 124
Pauling, Linus, 106
Pembroke, 19, 36, 40; lumber
    industry, 17, 40
Petawawa, CFB, 17
plutonium, 105, 114; Plutonium
    Pete, 47, 48
pointer (logging boat), 39
Pollard, W.G., 148
Pontecorvo, Bruno, 69
Potworowski, Andy, 148
Pringle, Peter, 147
Prosser, Bill, 52, 67

radioactivity, 46
radiation: alpha, beta, and gamma,
    46, 49; harmful effects , 49, 50;
    X-rays, 46

radium, 46
Rapides des Joachims, 40, 91,
    114
Renton, Ernie, 80, 83
Rickover, Admiral Hyman G., 96,
    97, 100, 122
Rideau River, 61
Robertson, J.A.L., 80, 132
Roentgen, Wilhelm, 46
Rolphton, 92
Roosevelt, Franklin D., 65, 66
Royal Society, 1999 statement, 143
Runnals, O.J.C., 146
Russians: Canada/Russia
    Agreement, 73; embassy, Ottawa,
    61, 72; alloy development 73-5

Sachs, Alexander, 65
Science Council of Canada, 148
Scott, Ted, Anglican Archbishop,
    150
Smith, Harold, 125
Smith, J. Herbert, 123; Agreement
    with AECL, 139
Smyth, Henry D., 136
SNC Lavalin, 135
Snow, C.P., 29
Solandt, Omand, 150
Spigelman, J., 147
Staff Hotel, Deep River, 22, 32
Steacie, E.W.R., 7
Steljes, John, 58, 59
Stranathan, James, 62
Strassmann, Fritz, 62
Szilard, Leo, 65, 66

Teller, Edward, 66
Thexton, Ted, 108
Tongue, Harold, 77

Tooley, Gerald, 27
tube alloys, 22
Tunnicliffe, Philip, 29

U-235, 88, 89
U.S. Atomic Energy Commission,
    101, 107, 146
U.S. Dept of Energy, 134
U.S. Nuclear Regulatory
    Commission, 135
U.S. Nuclear Submarine Program,
    96
Urey, H.C., 52
Ustinov, Peter, 29

van Arkel and de Boer zirconium,
    97
Veall, Norm, 70, 71
Vogel, Kenneth, 97

Walker, Joe, 41
Ward, A.G., 92
Weil, George, 69
Westinghouse, 96, 97
Wheeler, J.A., 65
Whitton, Charlotte, 16
Wigner, Eugene, 66
Williams, Murray, 76
Wilson, Willy, 113
Wolsung nuclear plant, Korea,
    139, 145
World Council of Churches, 149

ZEEP (Zero Energy
    Experimental Pile), 32, 53, 77
Zinn, Walter, 78, 79
Zircaloy-2, 98
zirconium, 97
Zirconium-niobium alloy, 73